TELLING STORIES

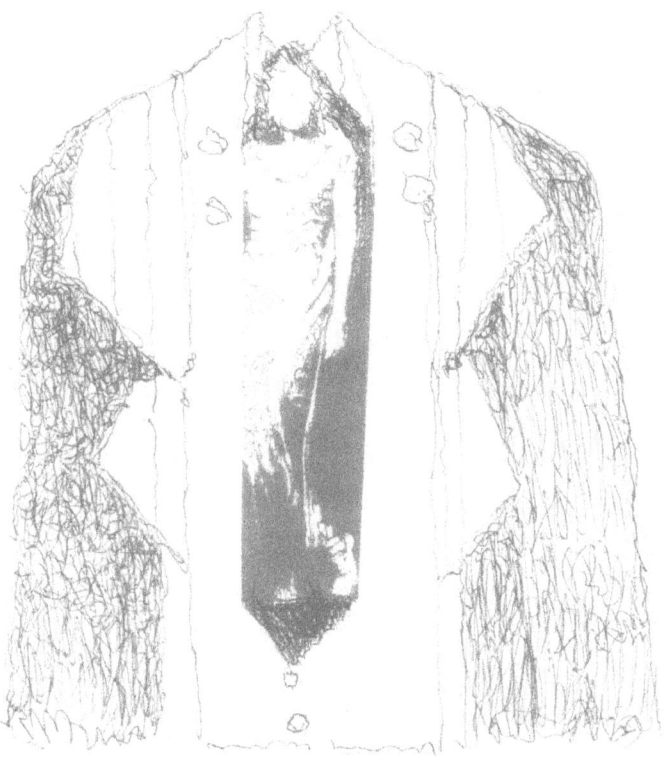

TELLING STORIES

This is dedicated to
Ace Ross Tyler Kim
without whose
assistance this
wouldn't be possible.

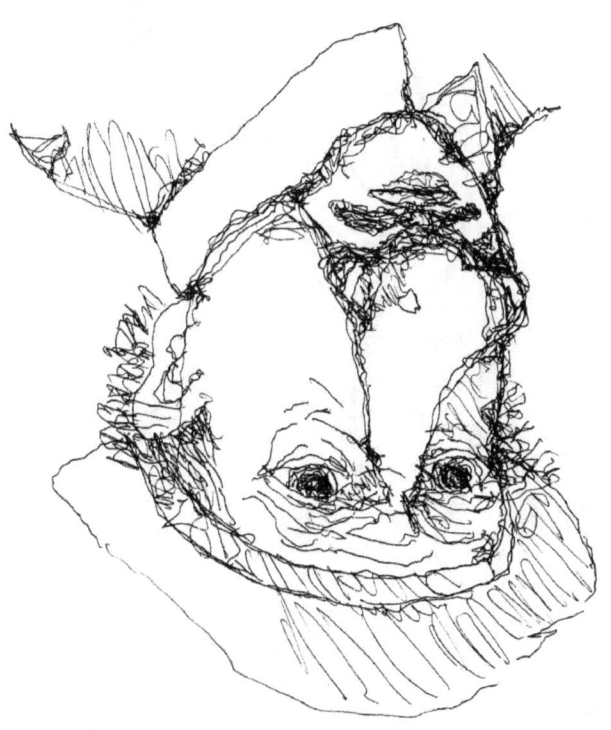

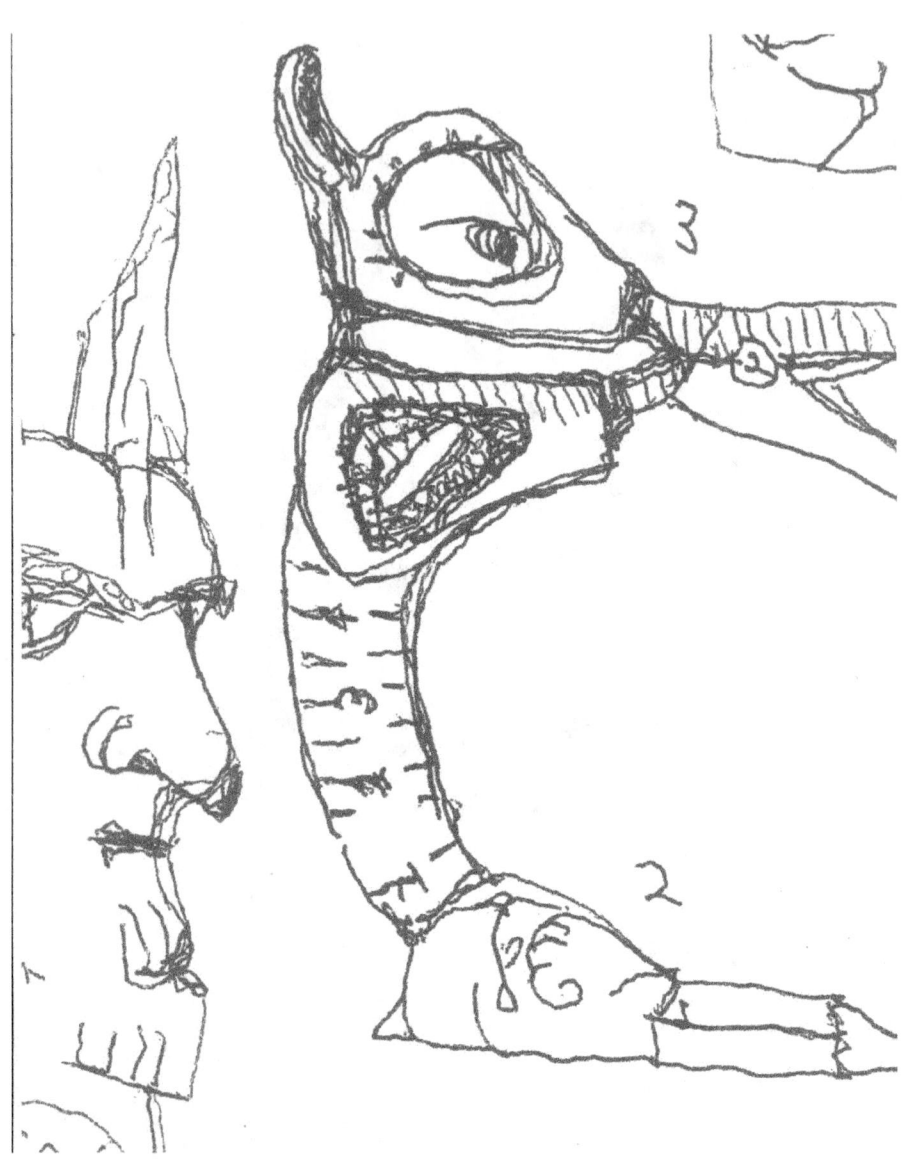

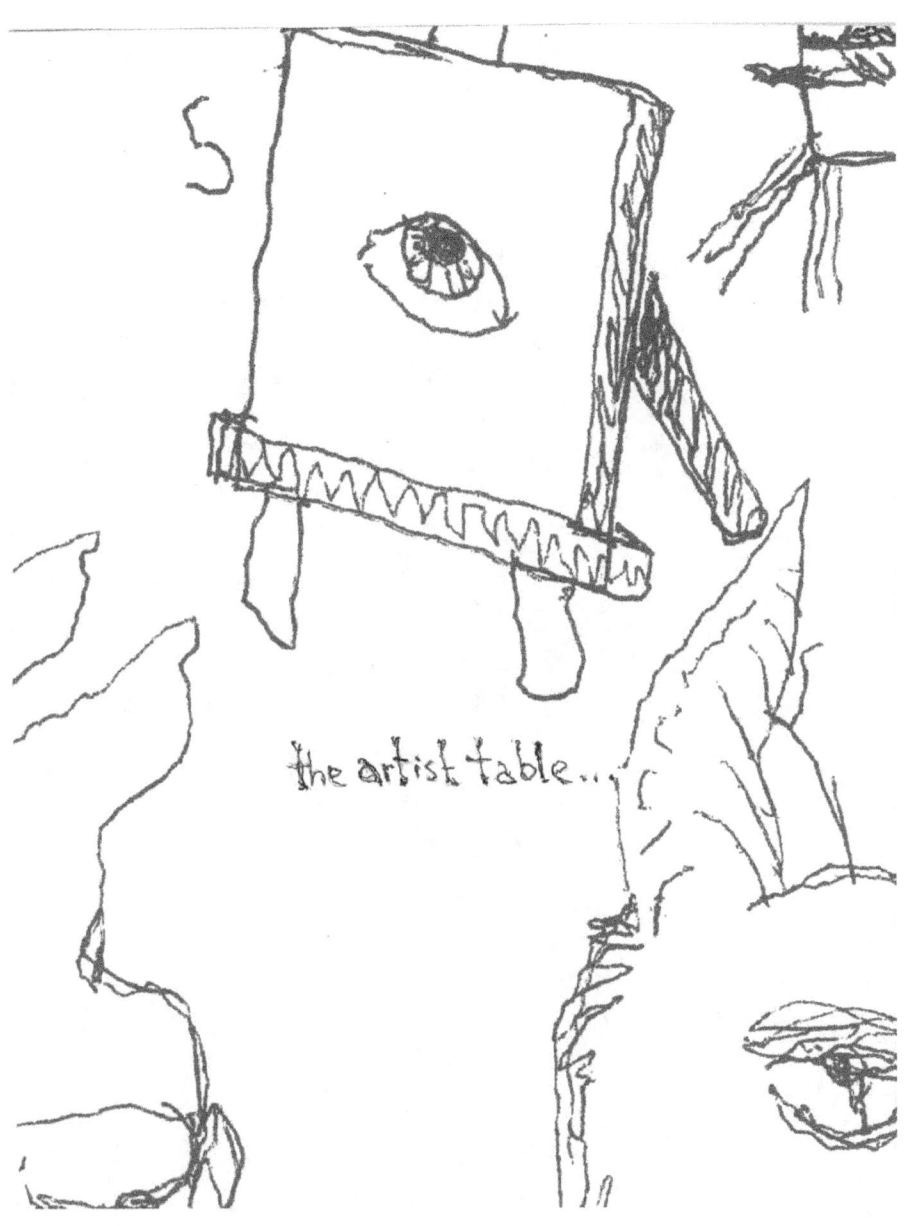

the artist table...

the eraser made a case
that there were some mistakes
that not only never should
have been made but that
the eraser was afraid
could not be taken away.

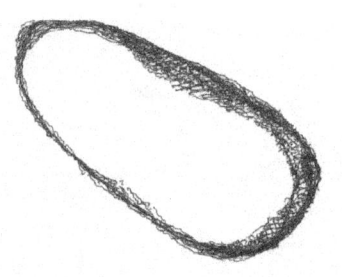

Then the,

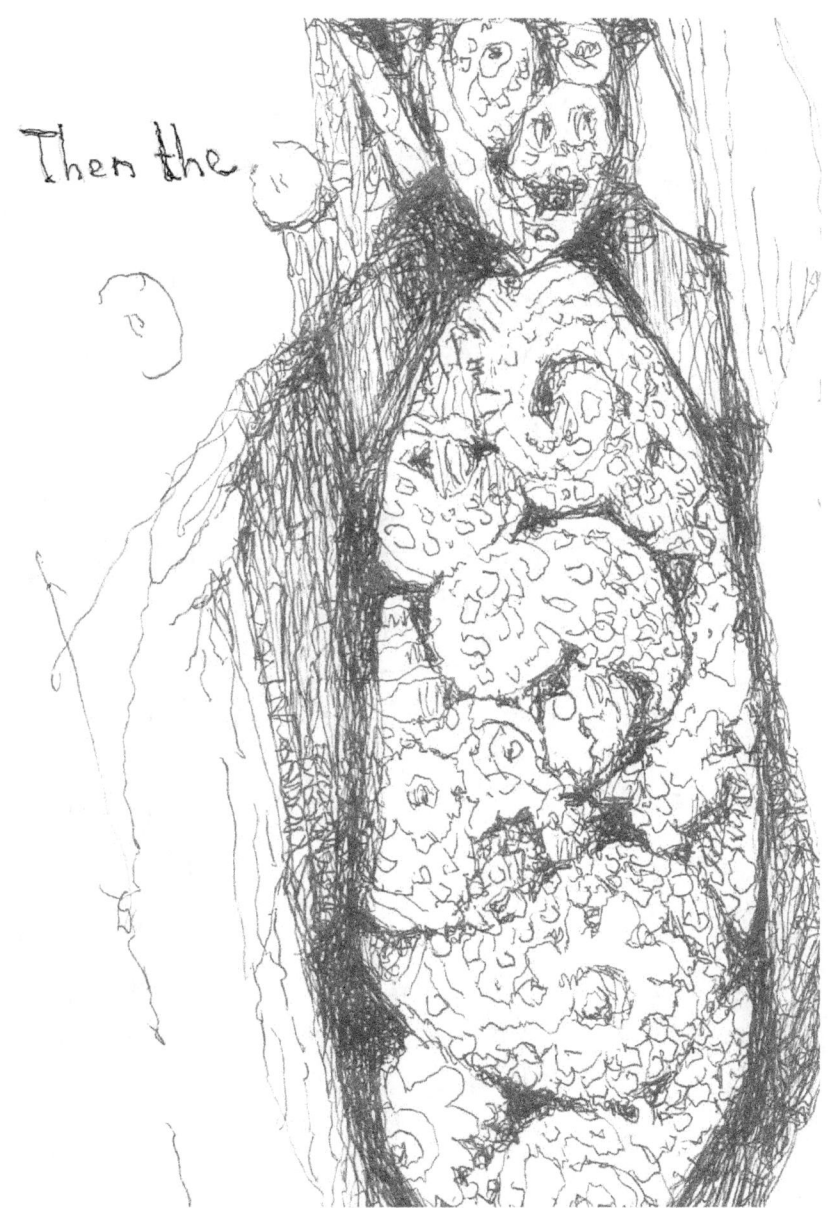

fat chalk court illustrator
wore a tie that was
as loud as he could..

..talk to the..

..JURY..

..who agreed..

12

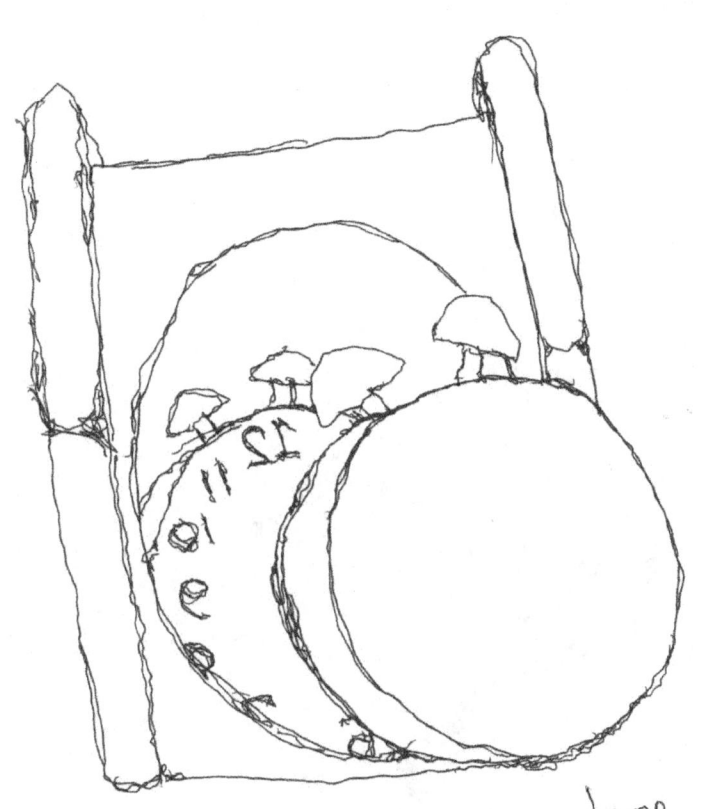

that anything done
could be undone
and that was the nature
of..

..everything that was.

And the eraser said,
" If I'm not mistaken."
And the chalk said,
" You're making a.."

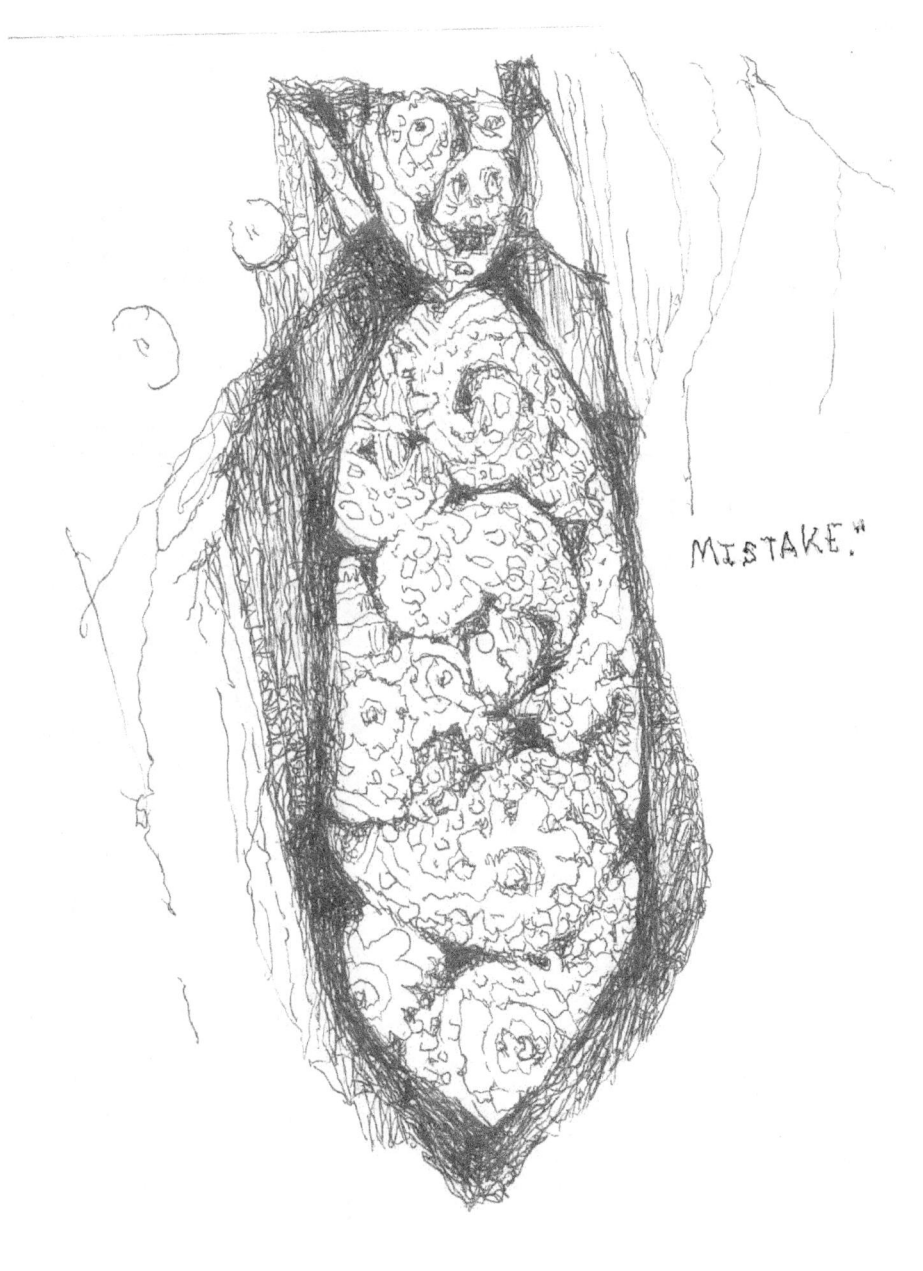

MISTAKE."

and the brushes
sang of parsley,
parsnips, and
potato cake.

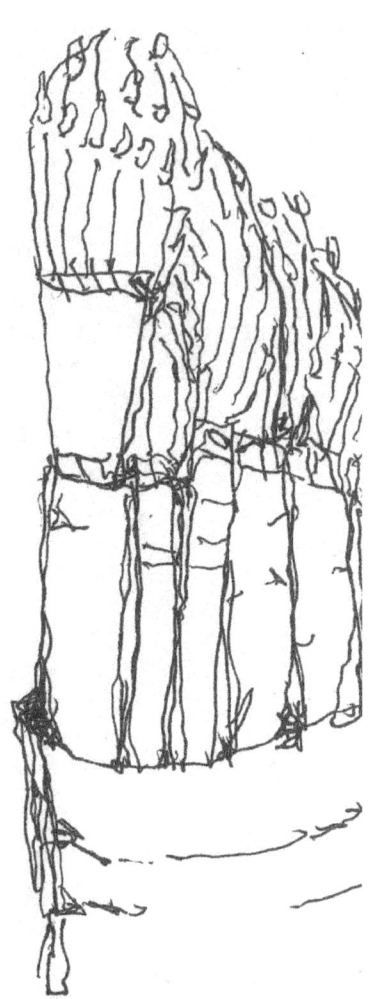

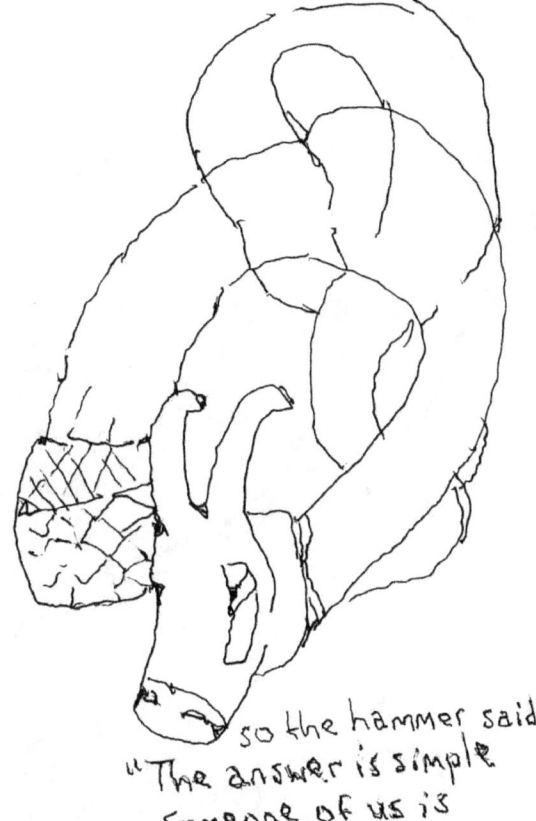

so the hammer said
"The answer is simple
someone of us is
to blame and the
answer is..

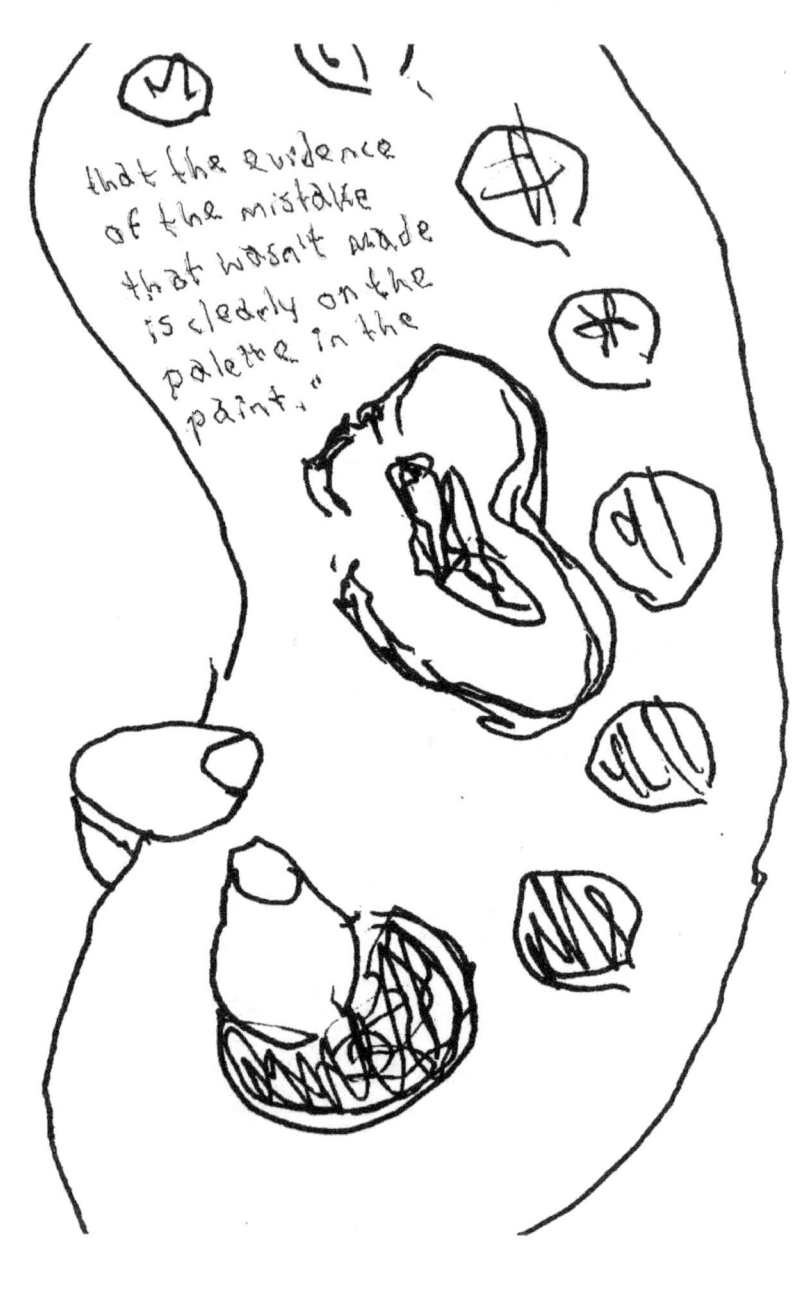

that the evidence
of the mistake
that wasn't made
is clearly on the
palette in the
paint."

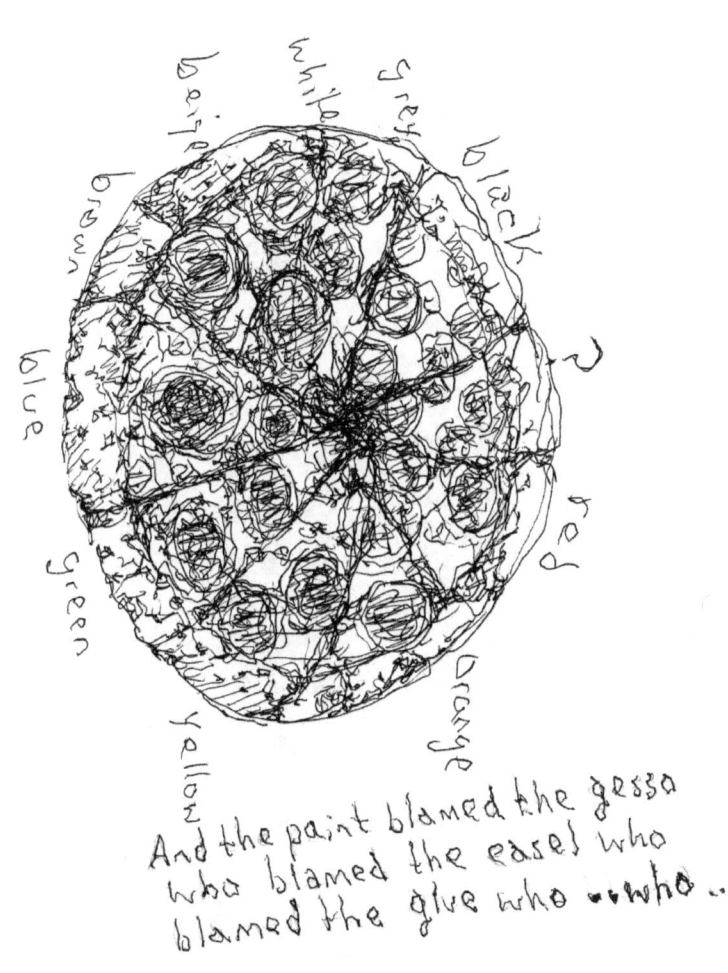

grey
black
white

red

beige
brown

orange

blue

yellow

green

And the paint blamed the gessa
who blamed the easel who
blamed the glue who ..who..

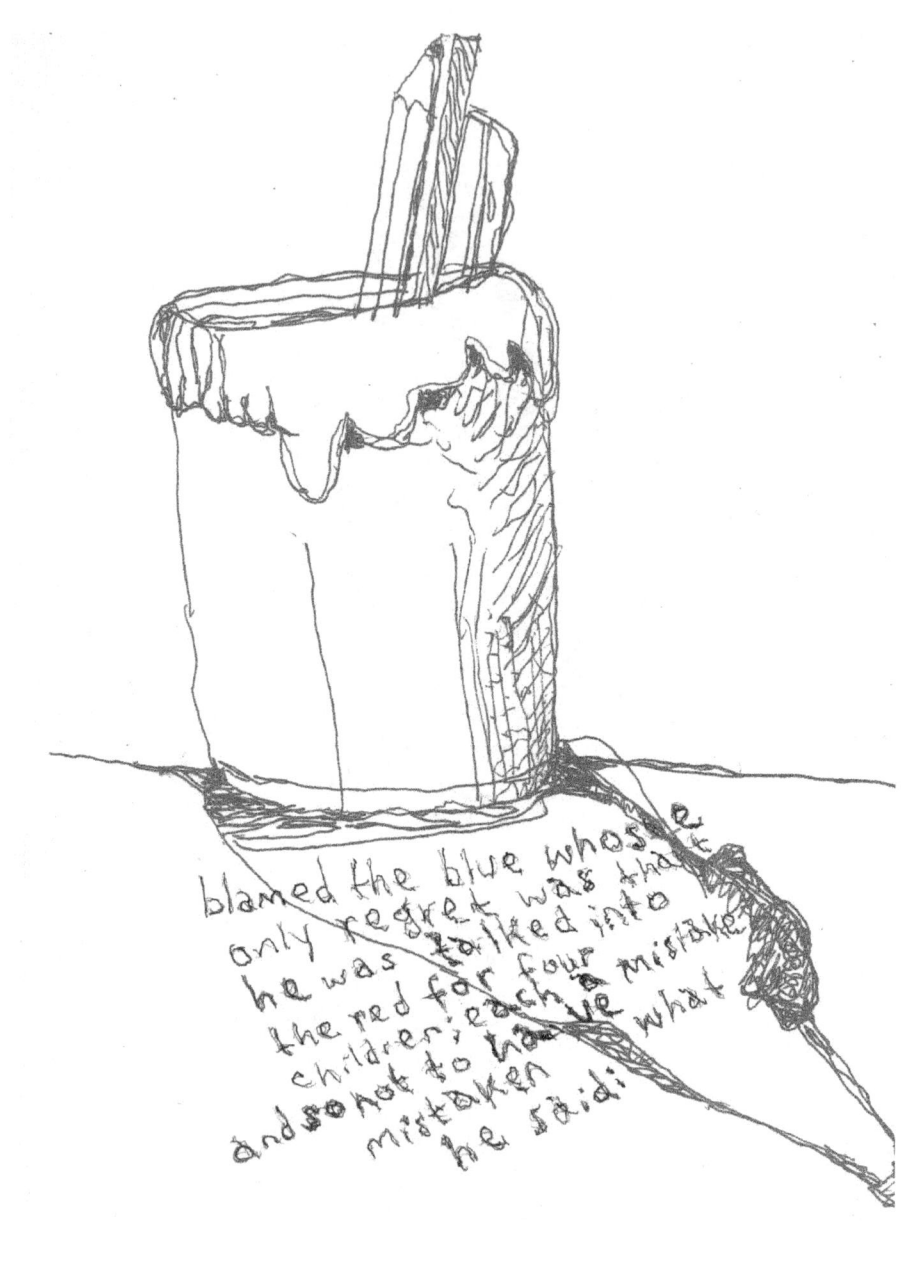

blamed the blue whose
only regret was that
he was talked into
the red for four
children; each a mistake
and so not to have what
mistaken
he said

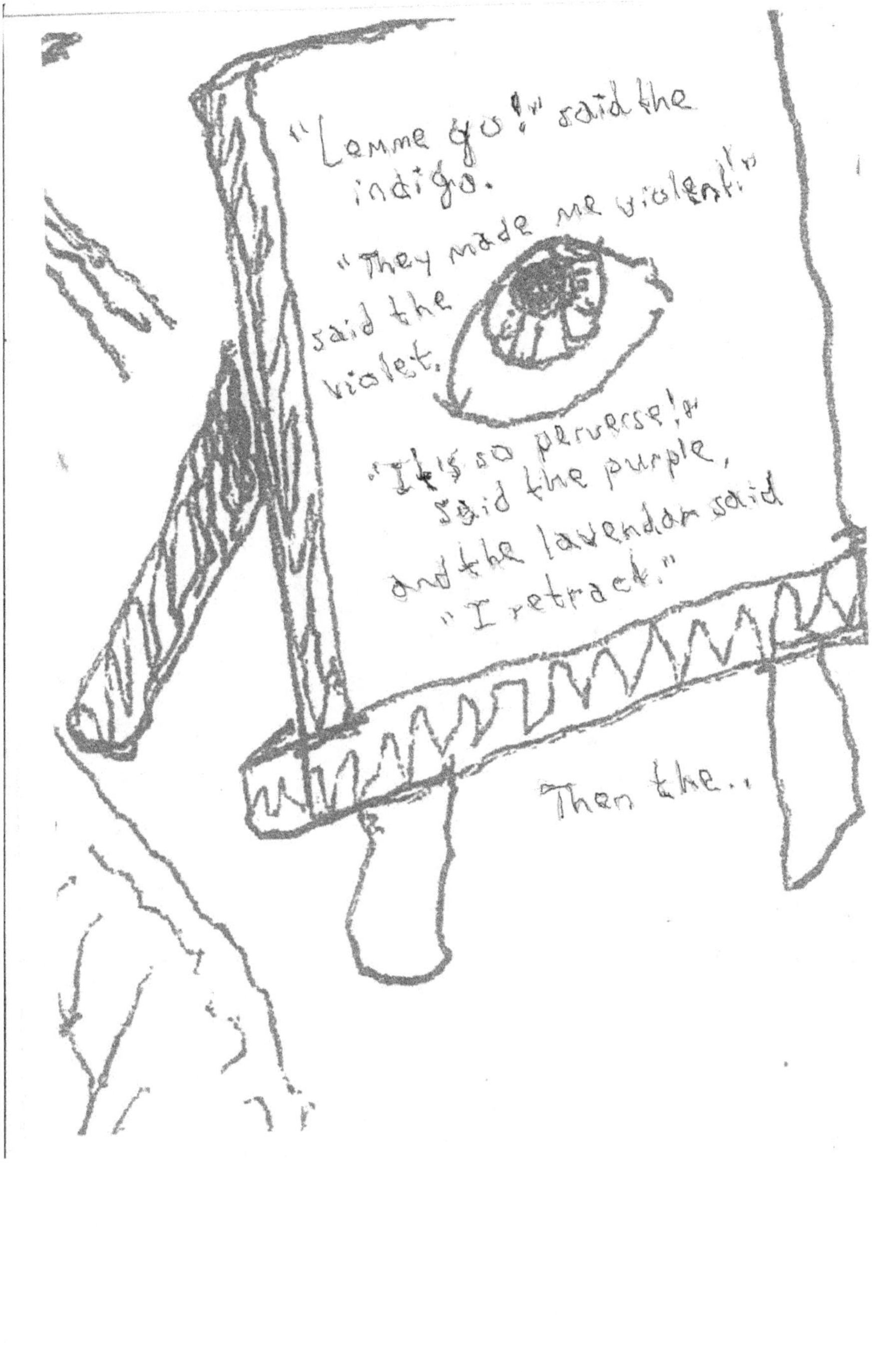
"Lemme go!" said the indigo.
"They made me violent!" said the violet.
"It is so perverse!" said the purple, and the lavendar said "I retrack."
Then the..

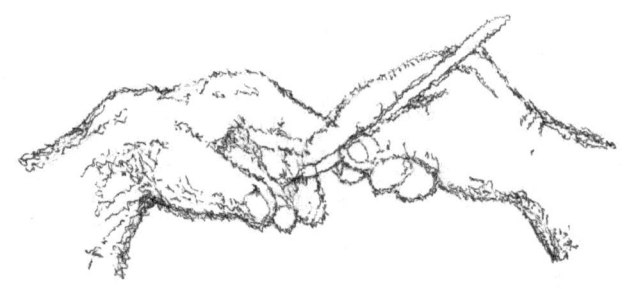

brushes sang a song
from the filbert to
the flat about Picasso,
Michelangelo and
Rembrandt that went:
"I am the brush that
knew the brunch that
changed the face

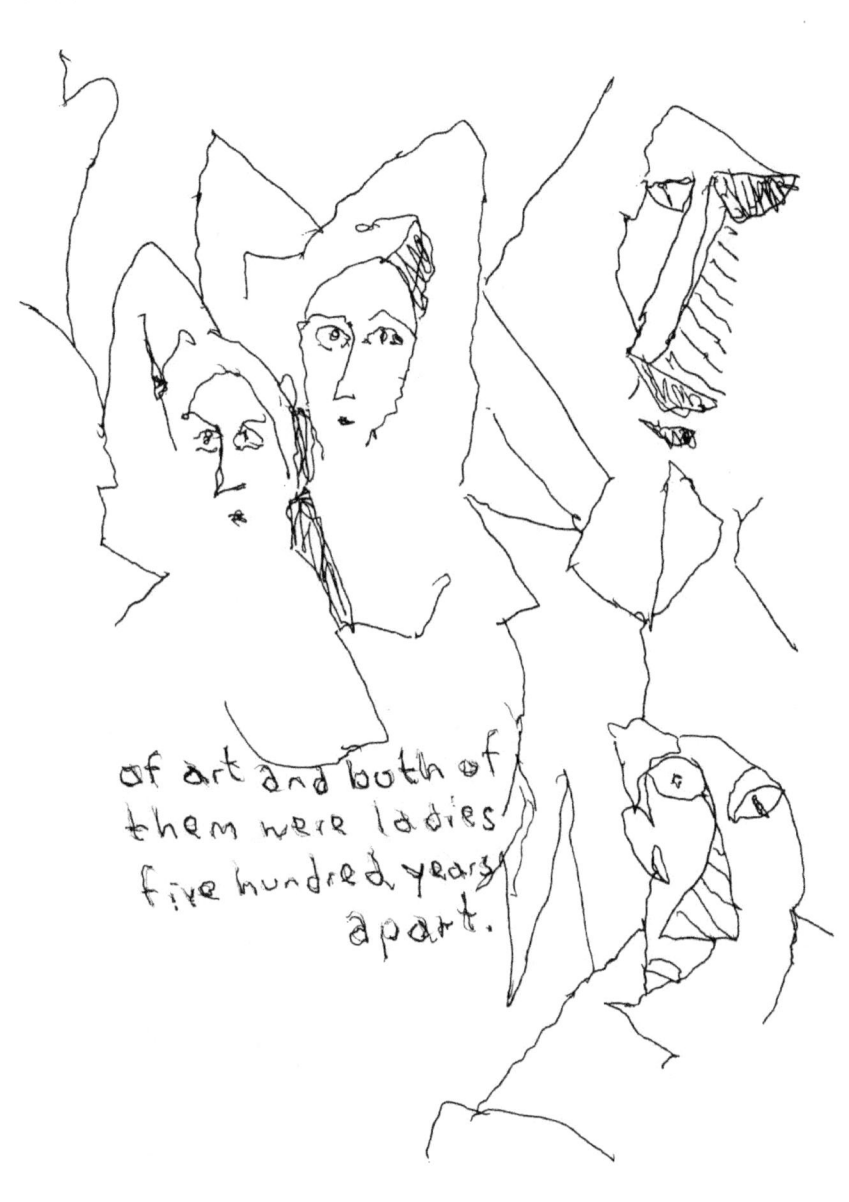

of art and both of
them were ladies
five hundred years
apart.

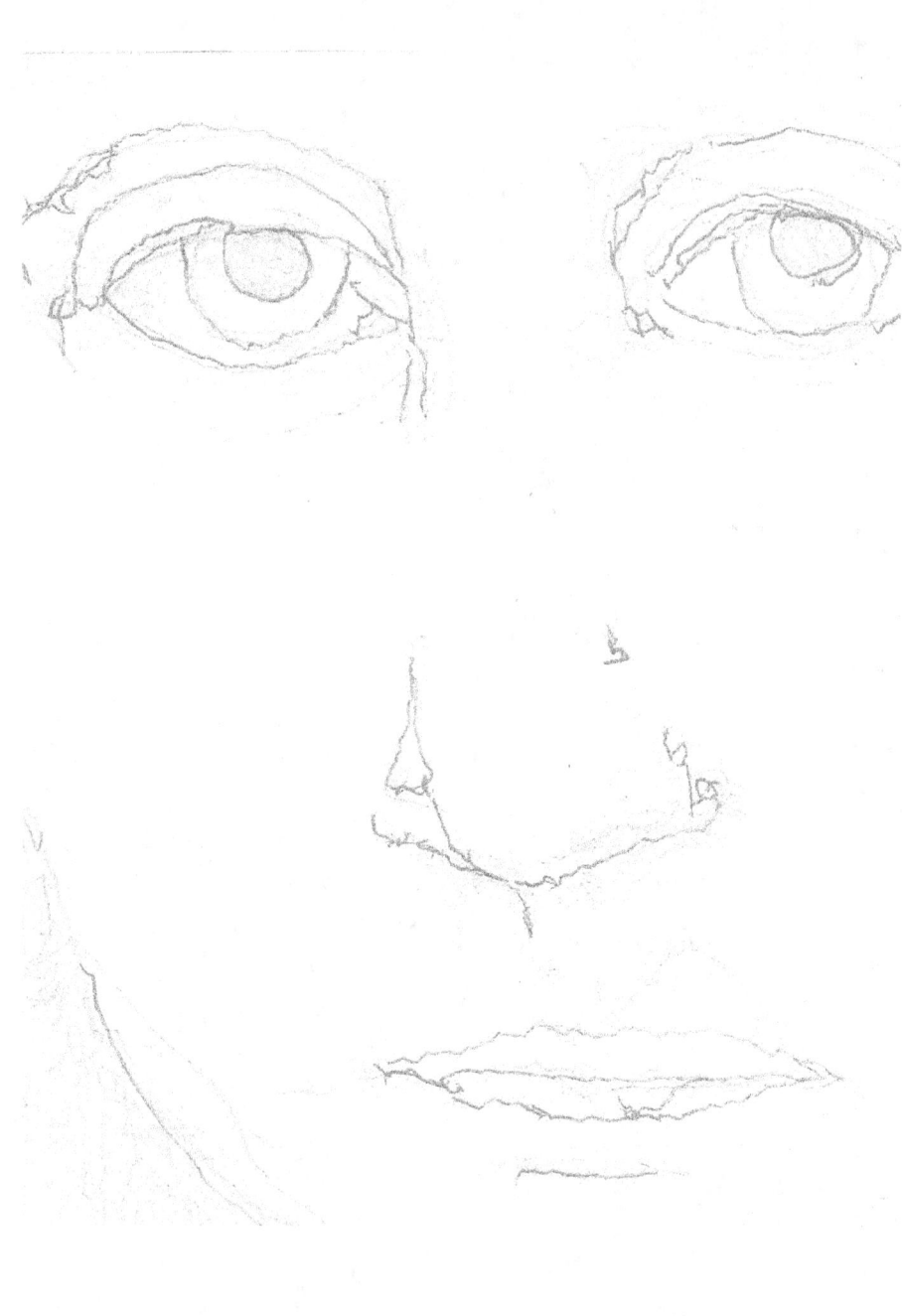

And I can paint a fountain by that second to last Italian so you'd appreciate the feat.

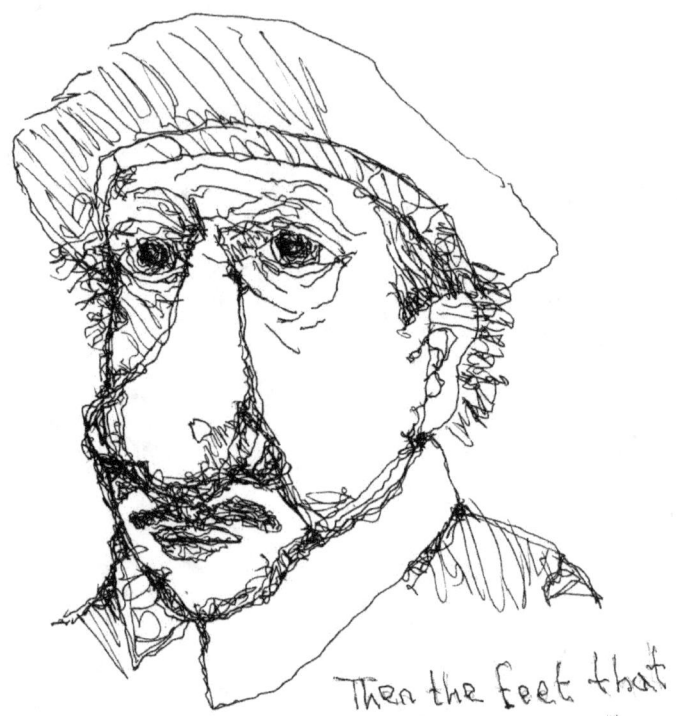

Then the feet that smellet so awful said, "It smells like a mistake to me."

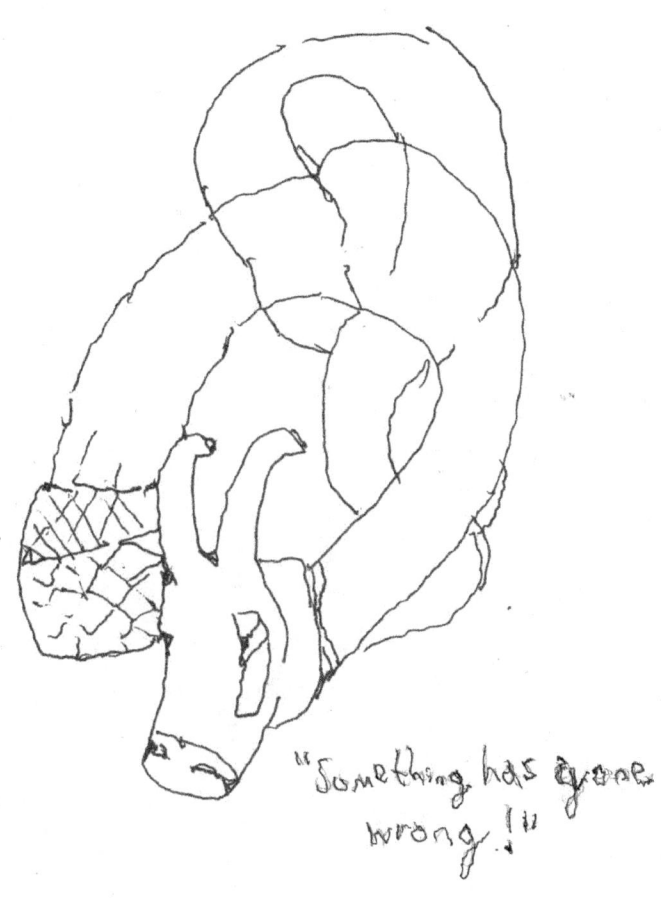

"Something has gone wrong!"

"NOT NECESsacerily.

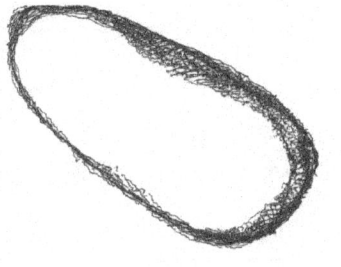

and the brushes
sang of
pimento,
impasto
and
chiaroscuro...
tint.

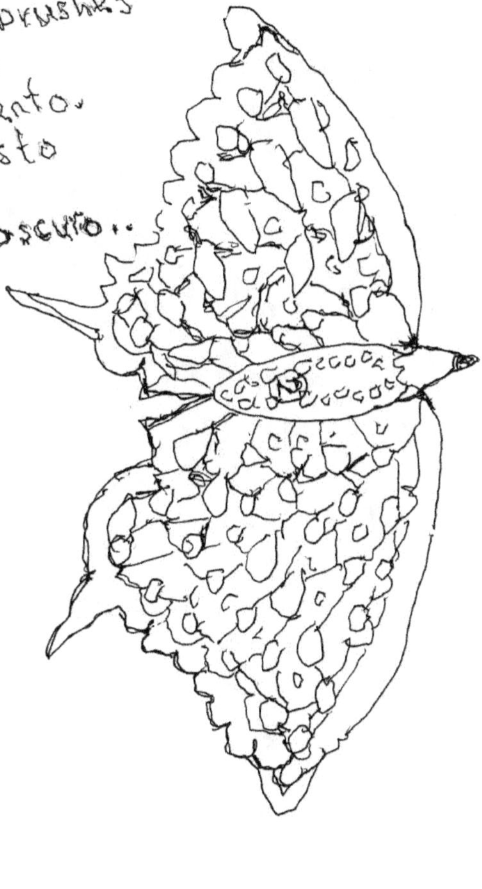

and the appelate judge said.
"So from the Italian it means
snapped in half, thrown
away or melted in a Kiln?"

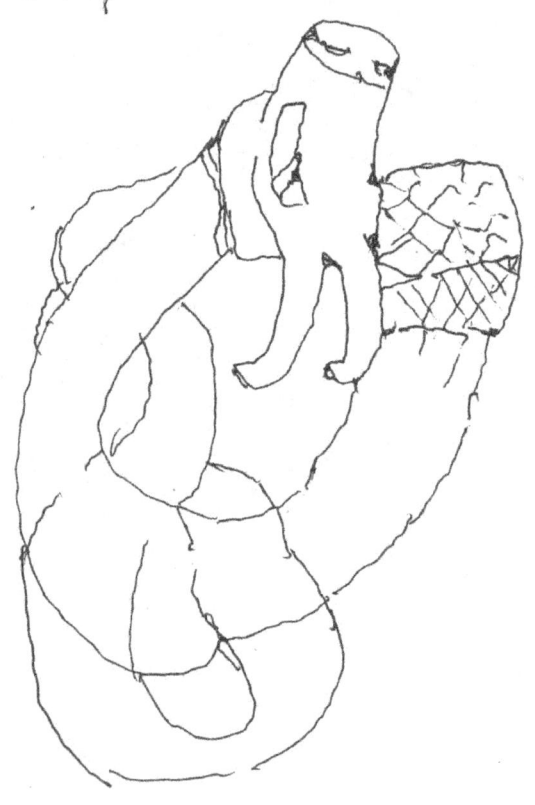

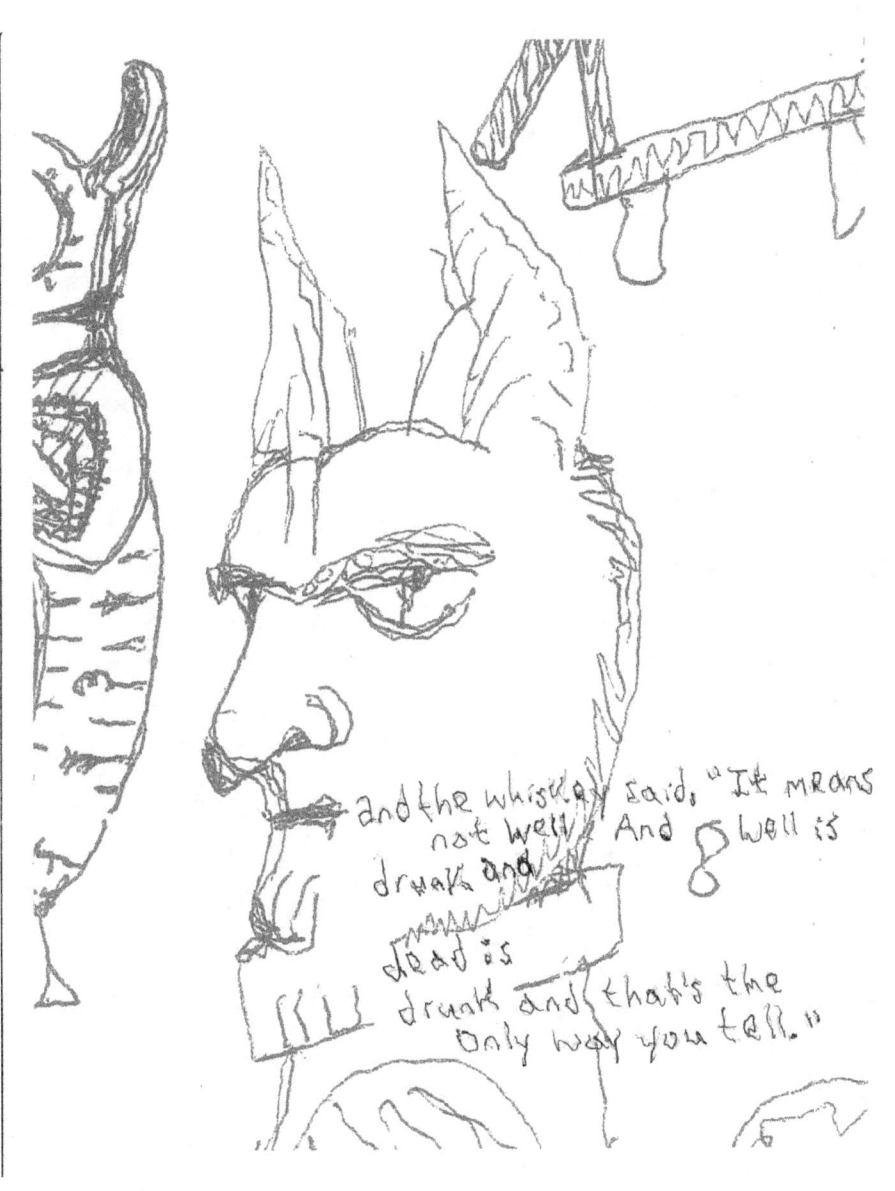

and the whiskey said, "It means not well. And well is drunk and dead is drunk and that's the only way you tell."

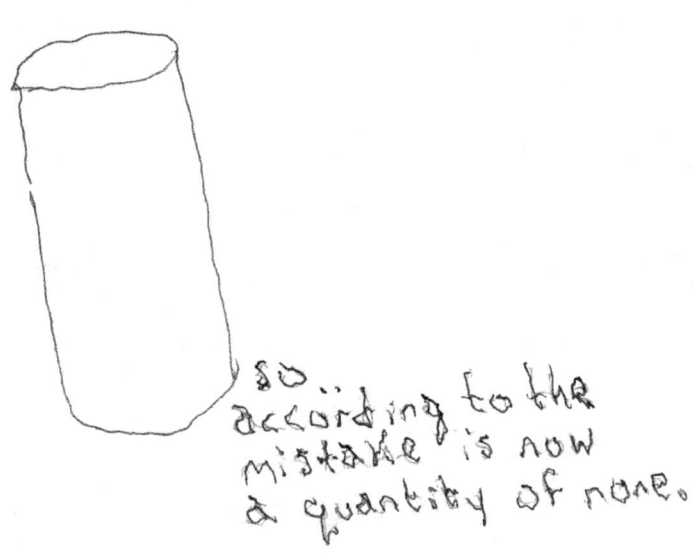

so...
according to the
mistake is now
a quantity of none.

in other words,

"It's gone."

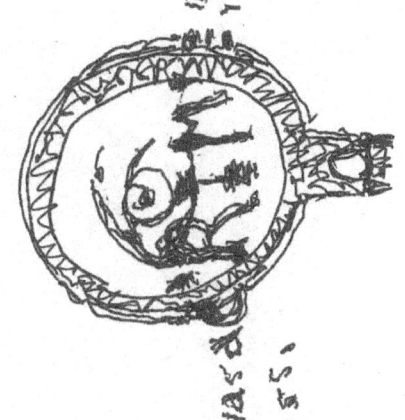

"said the magnifying

"It was glass,"

glass.

that's what you get without
rules..

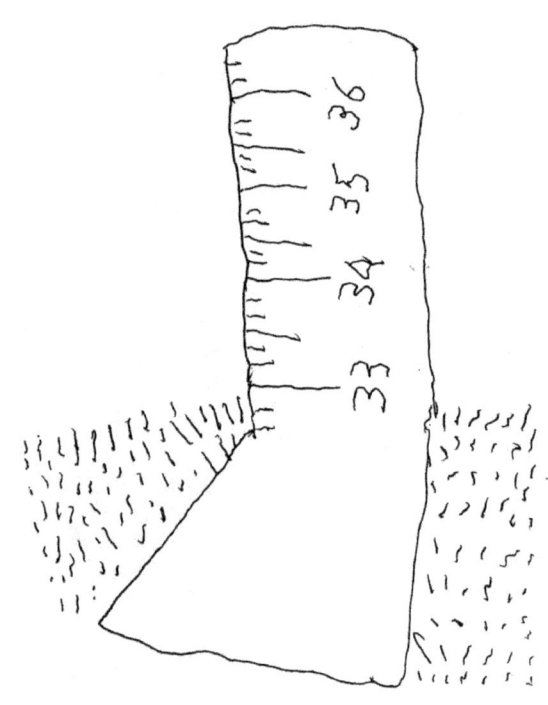

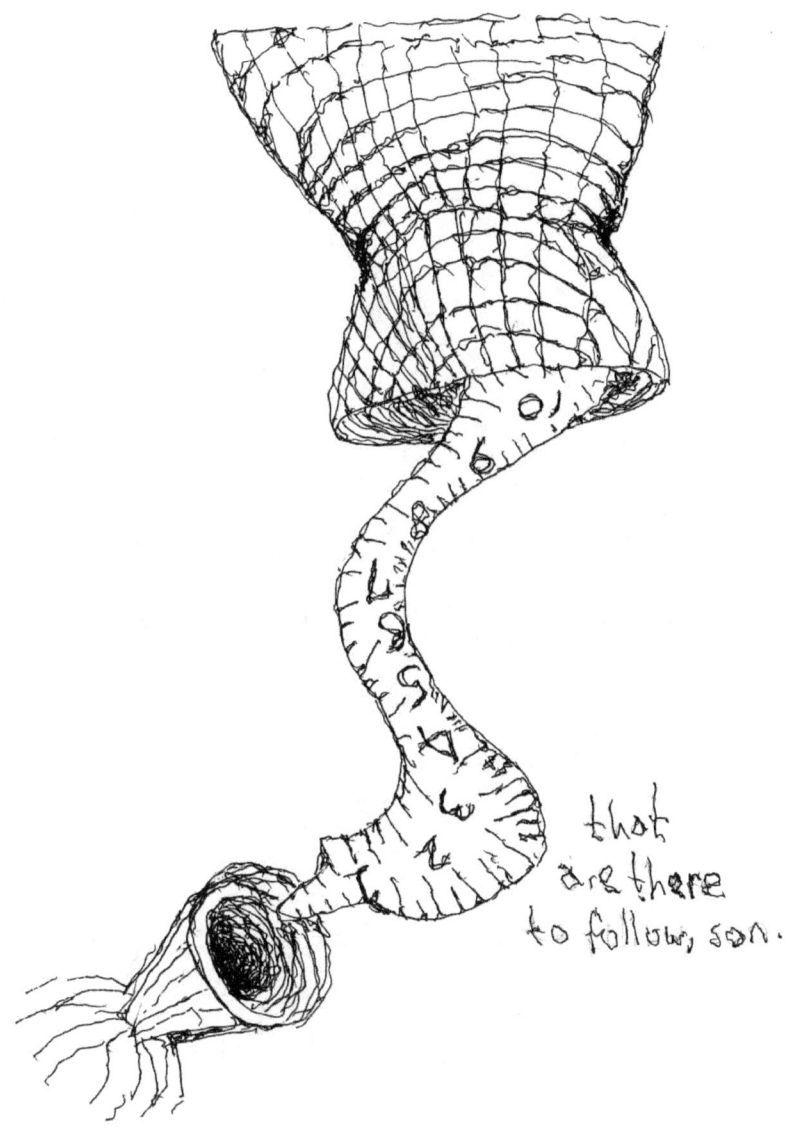

that
are there
to follow, son.

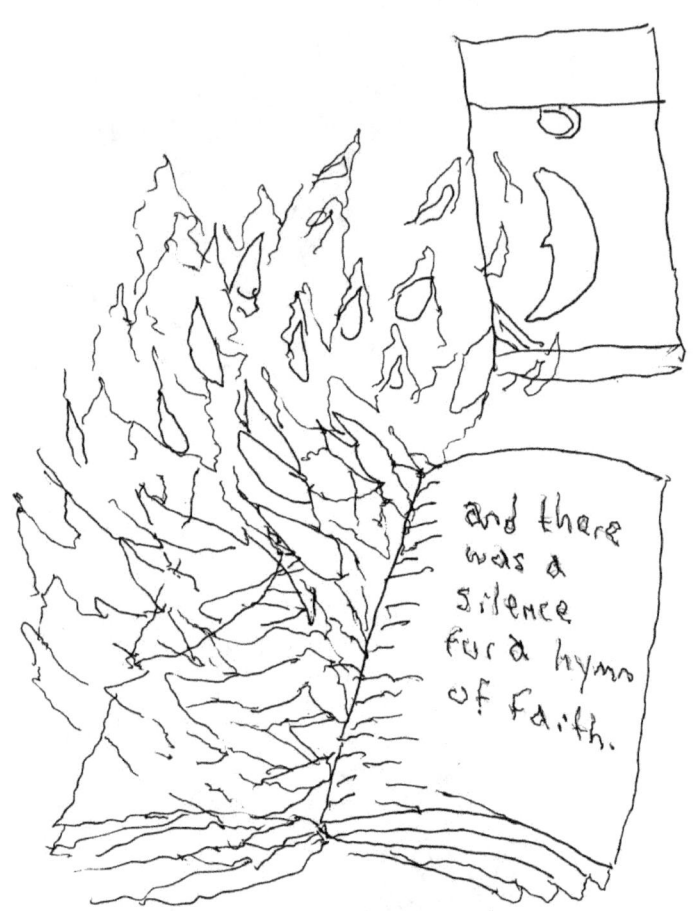

and there
was a
silence
for a hymn
of faith.

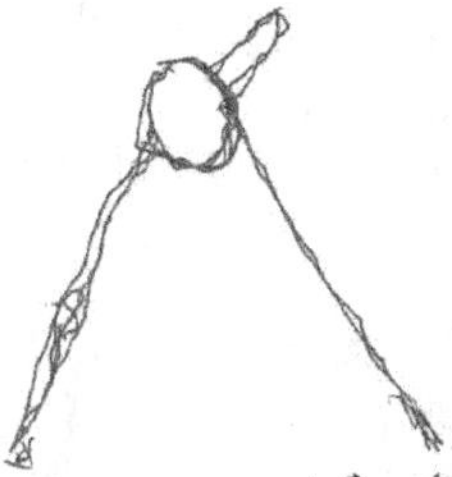

"This wouldn't be
as well written
if it didn't
come with pictures,"
said the fixtured
frame.

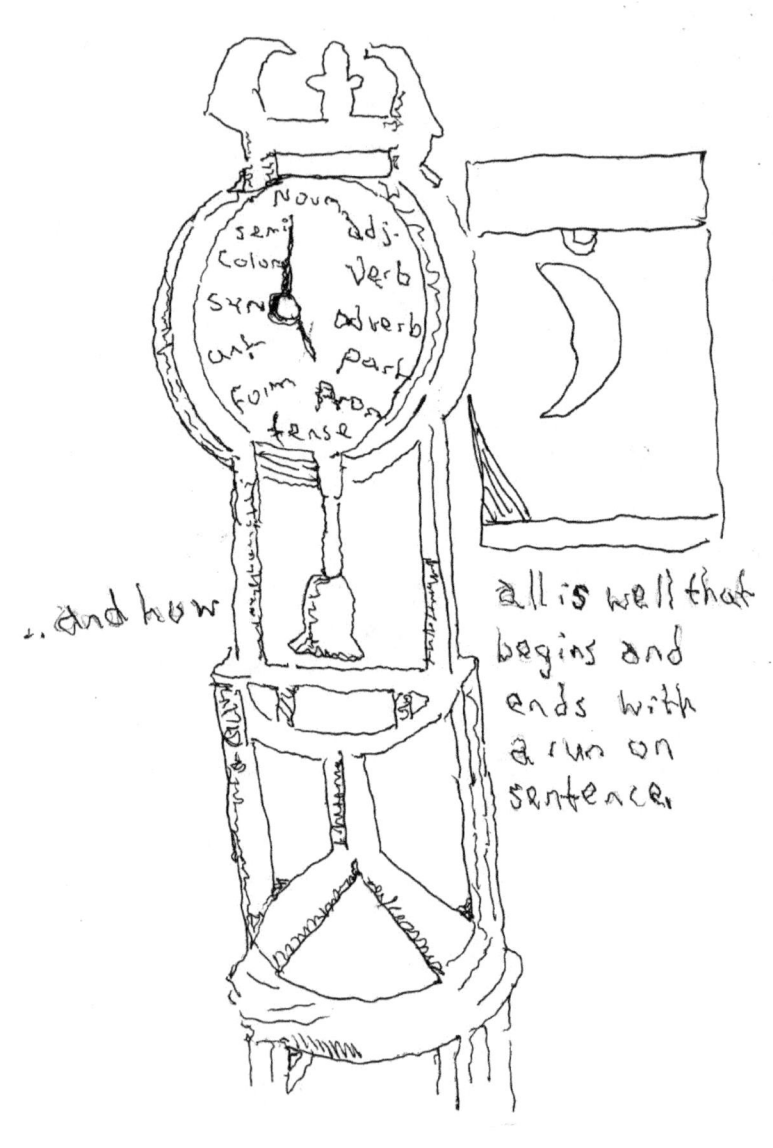

..and how

all is well that
begins and
ends with
a run on
sentence

when
there was a
song about
how comfortable
the thought
of nothing..

.. I S on the brushes.

and that is when the whiskey
did what no artist
aid had ever done.

He cried for that
mistake.

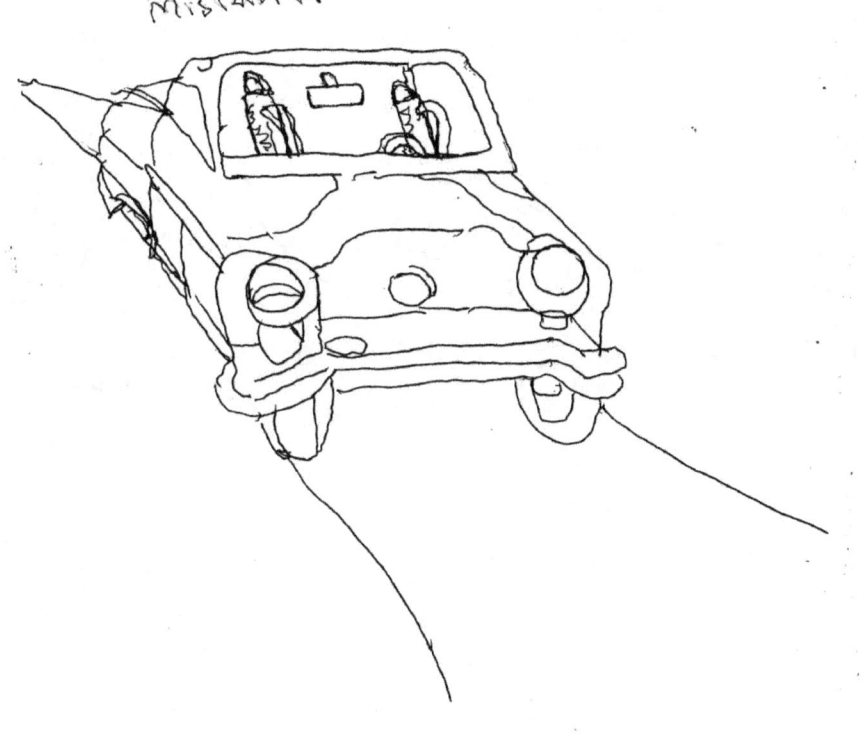

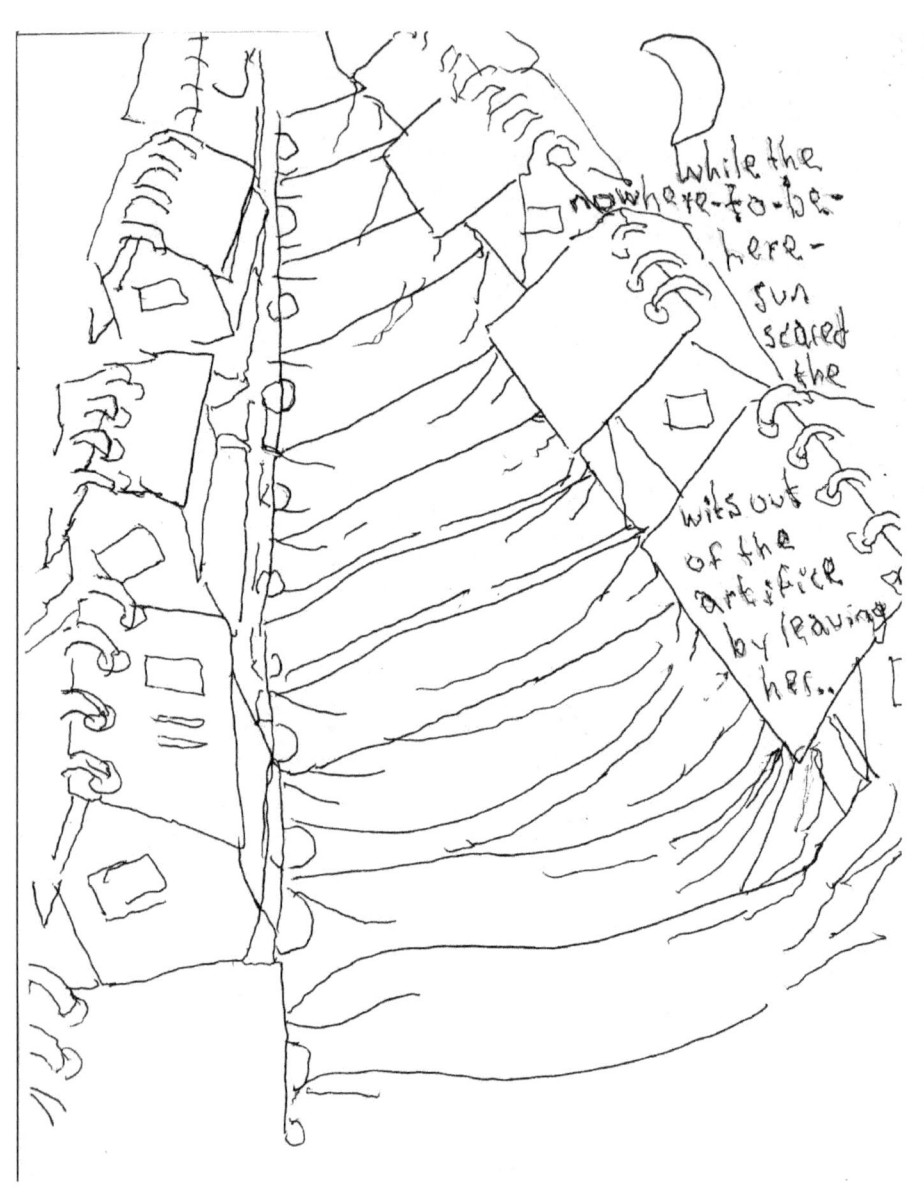

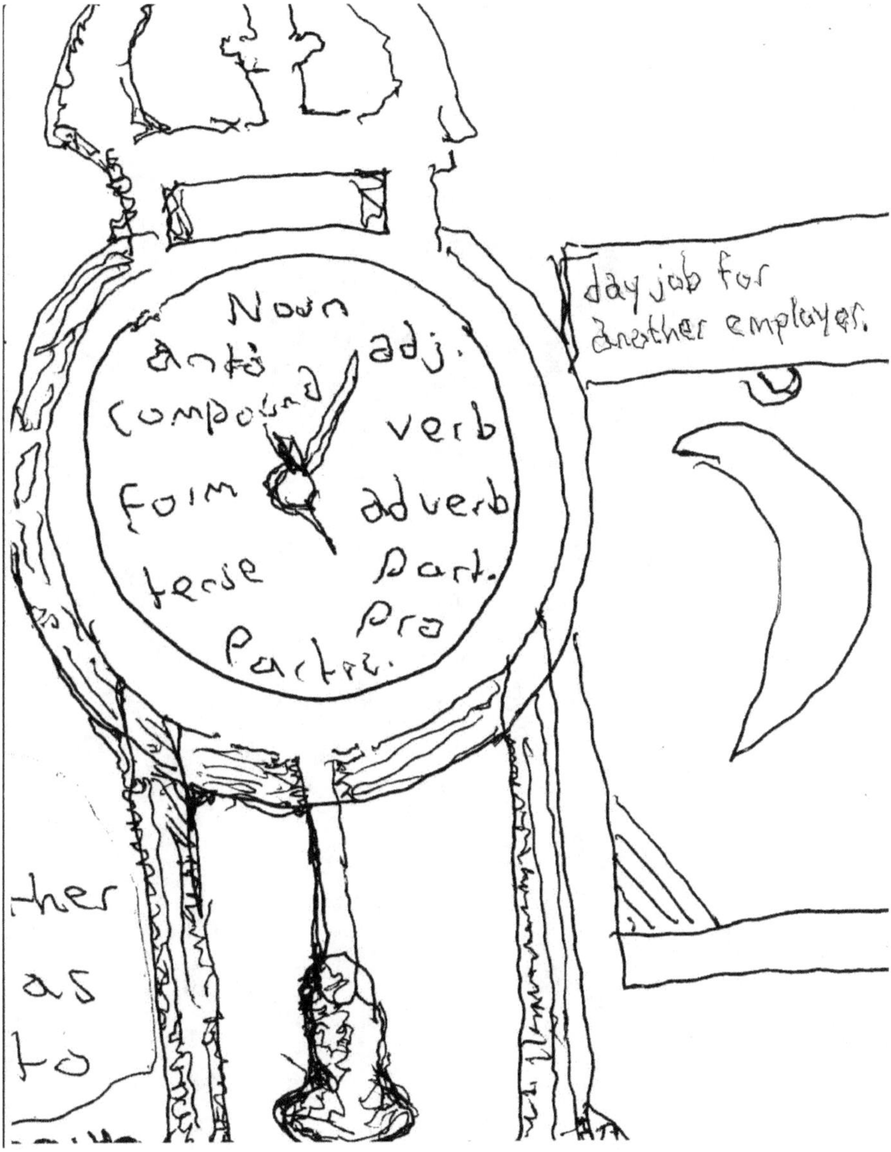

Noun
anti adj.
Compound verb
form adverb
tense part.
Pro
Partic.

day job for
another employer.

ther

as

to

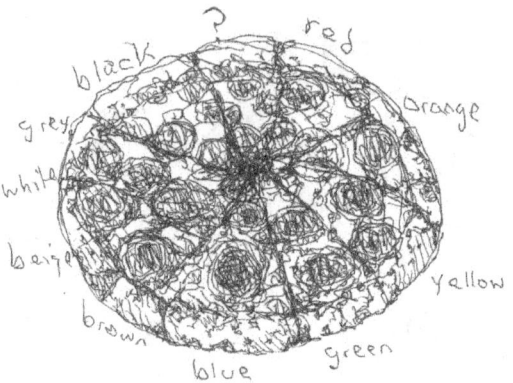

And the hammer said, "In the matter of the mistake my decision is.. a sentence is a line up of words that are a cast of characters that tell a story that wouldn't mean the same in any other..

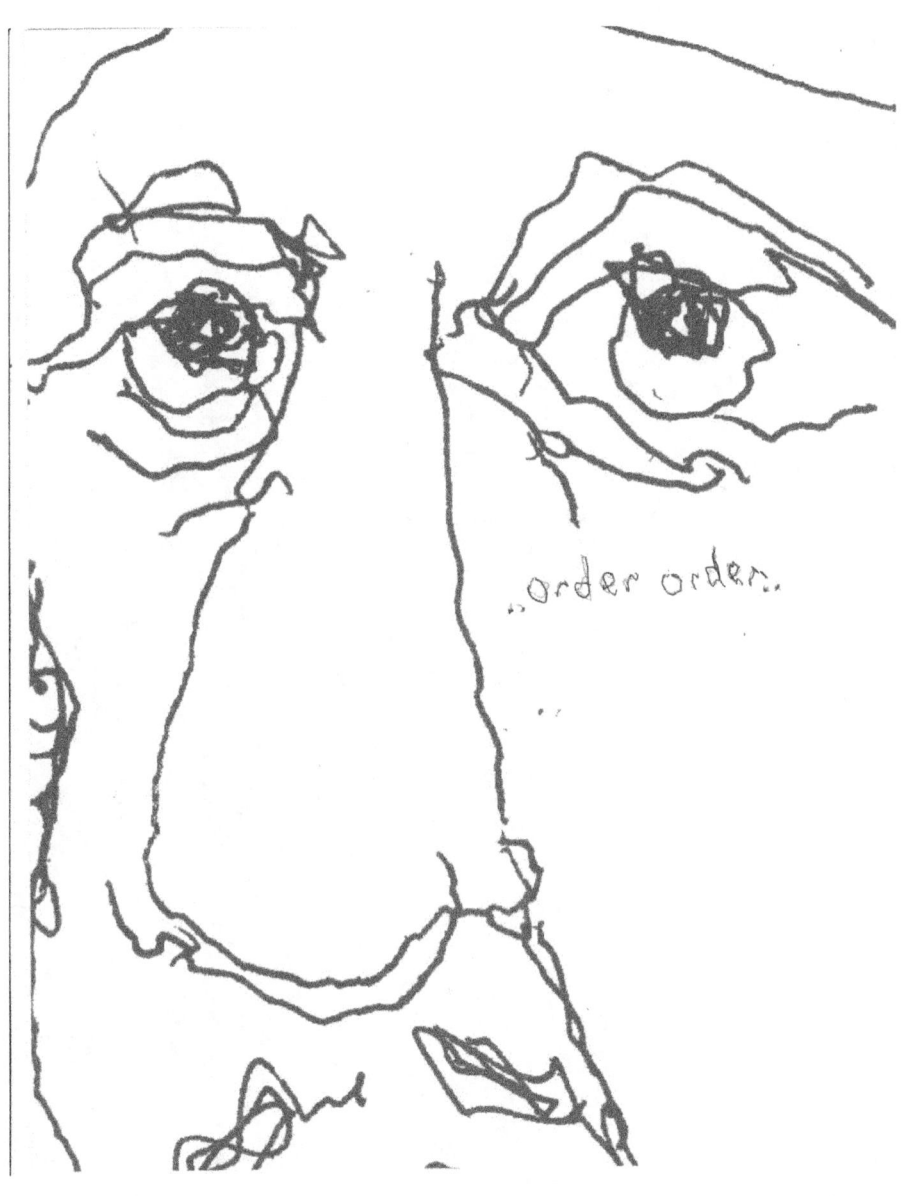

„order order.

ORDER!"

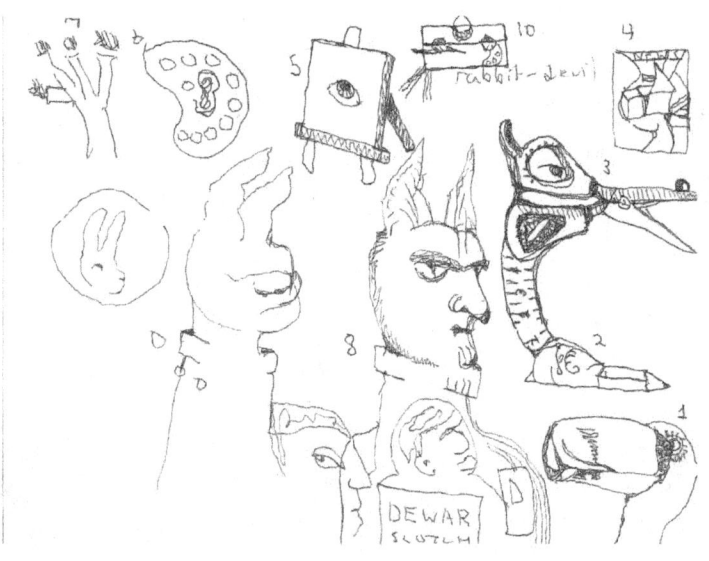

There are those who know
    this couldn't have happened,

That the almanac can't cure
the weather, that you can't see
infinity in a barber's mirror an'
that forever's not forever
                            but we
                            know
                            better...

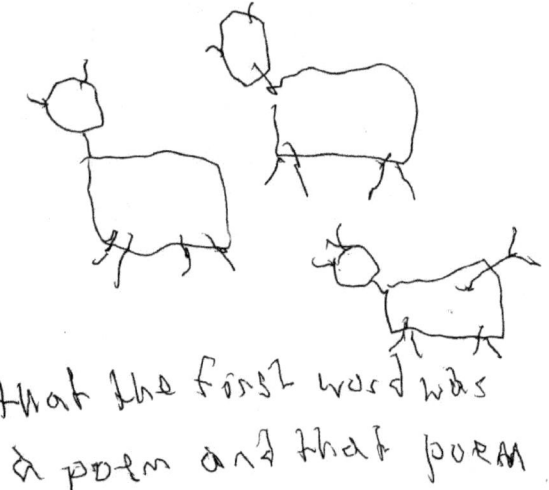

that the first word was
a poem and that poem
was a picture.-

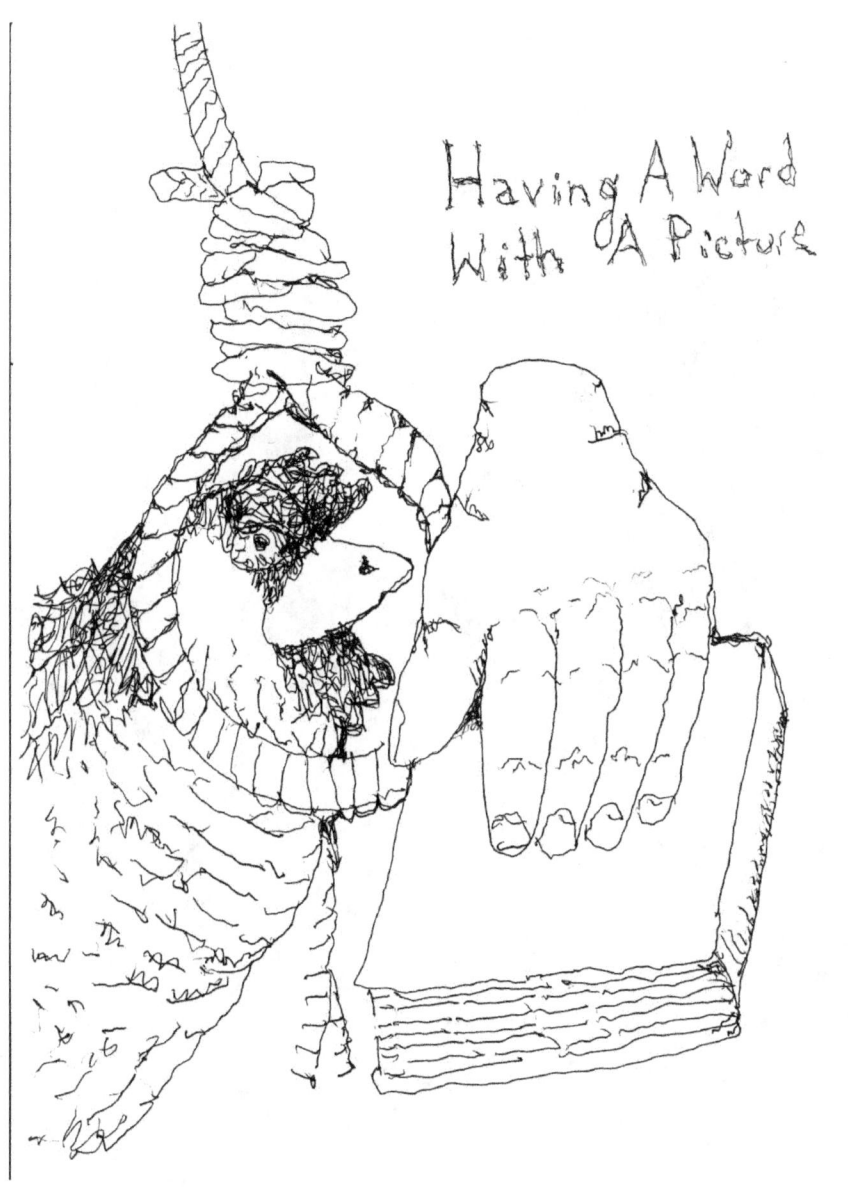

Having A Word
With A Picture

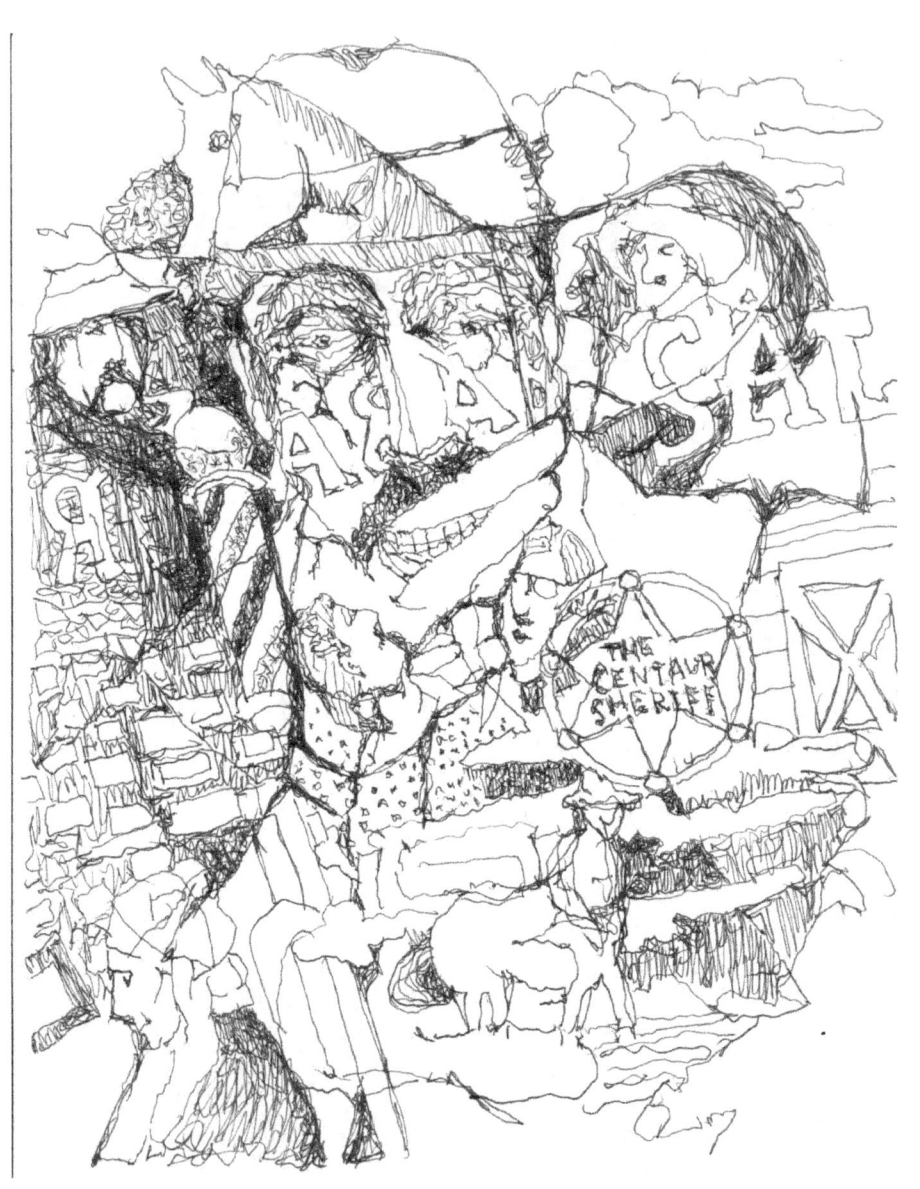

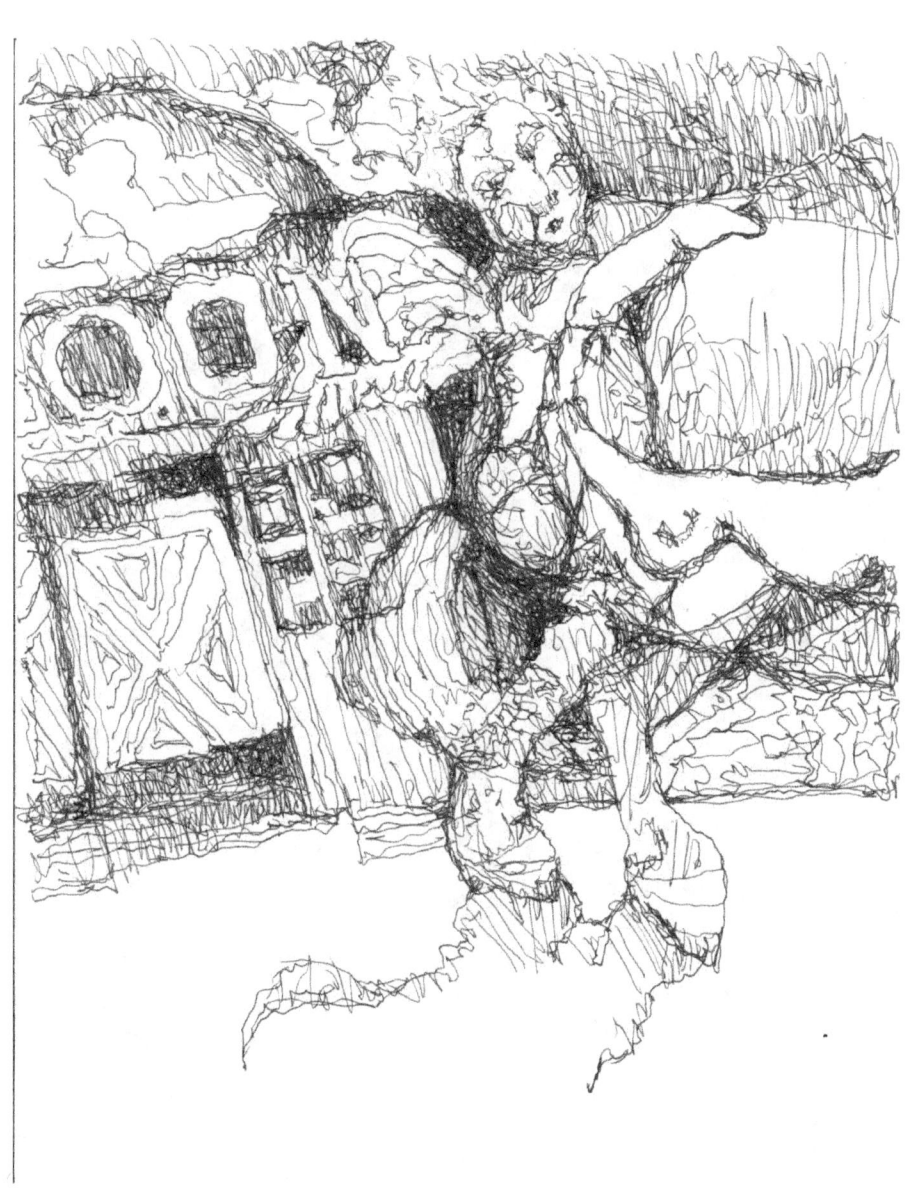

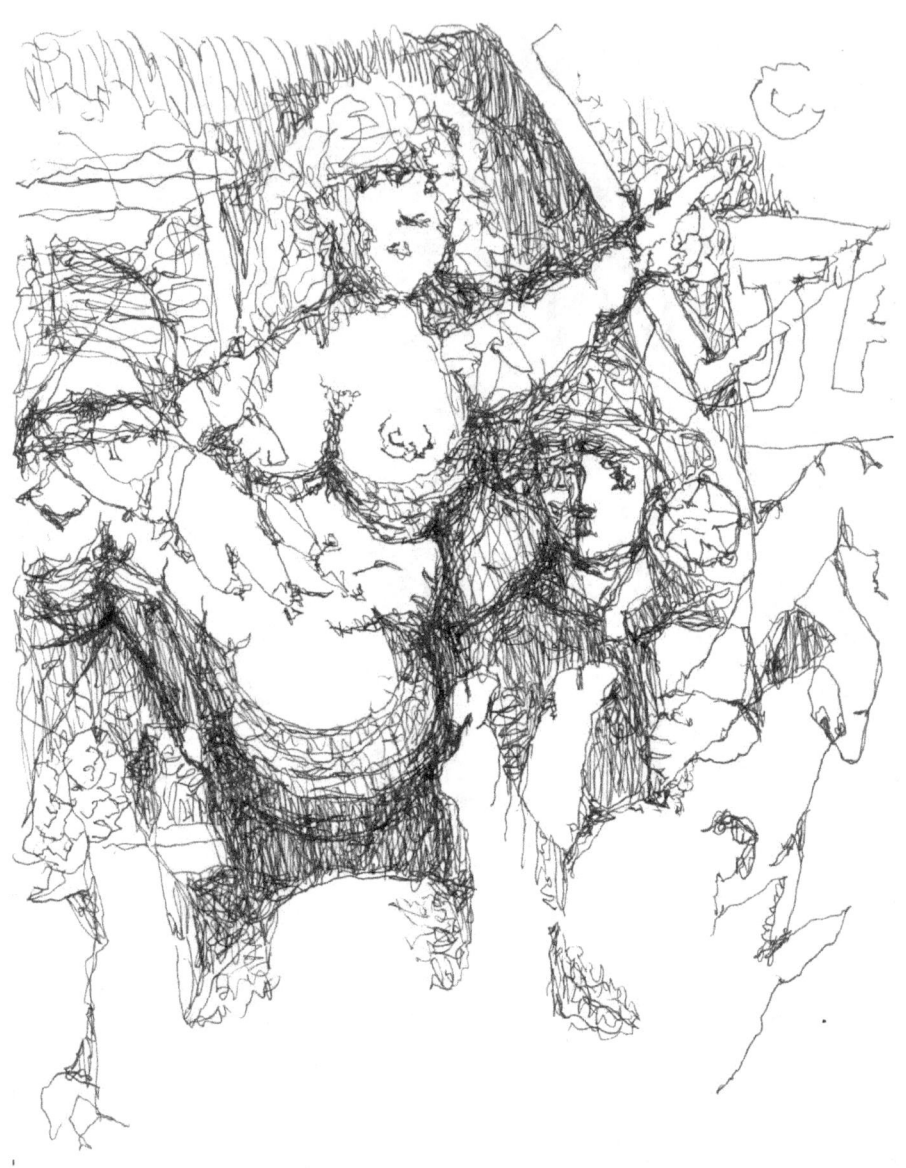

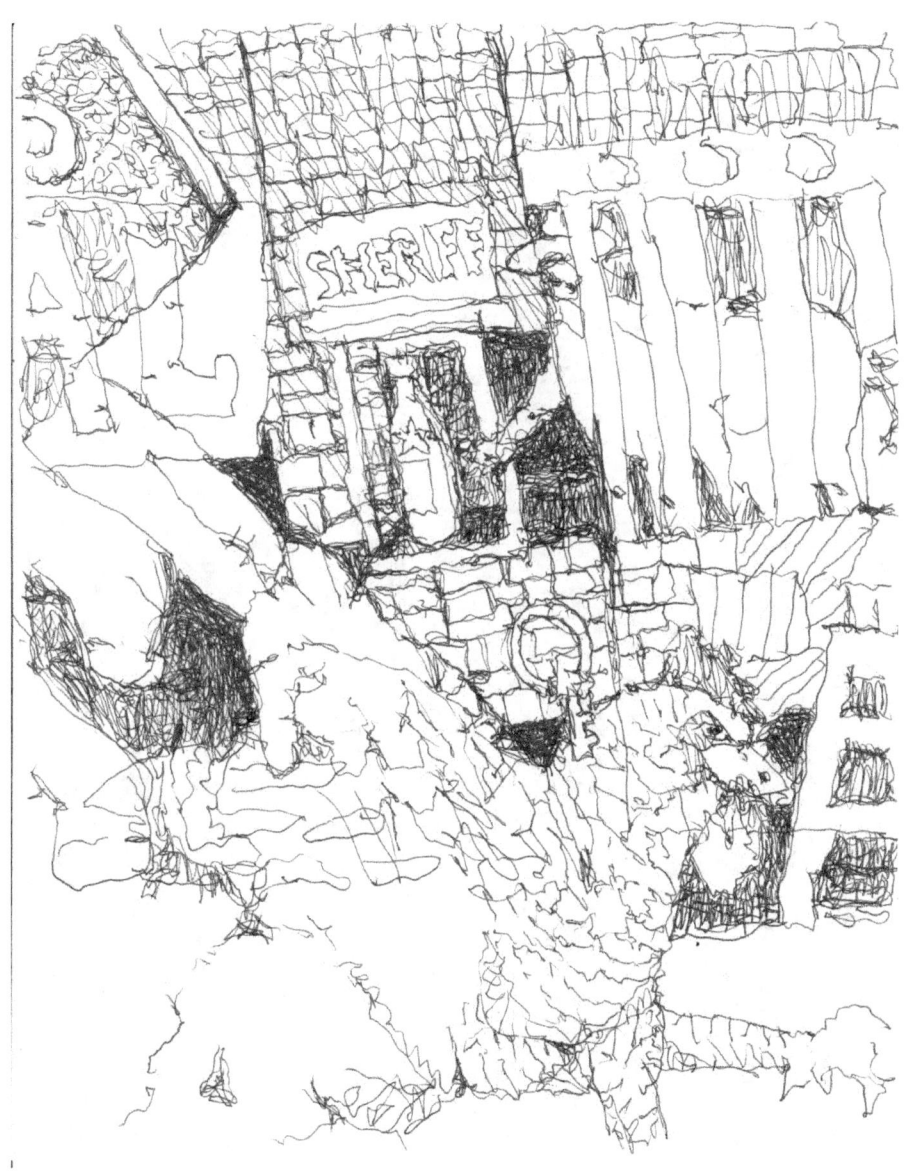

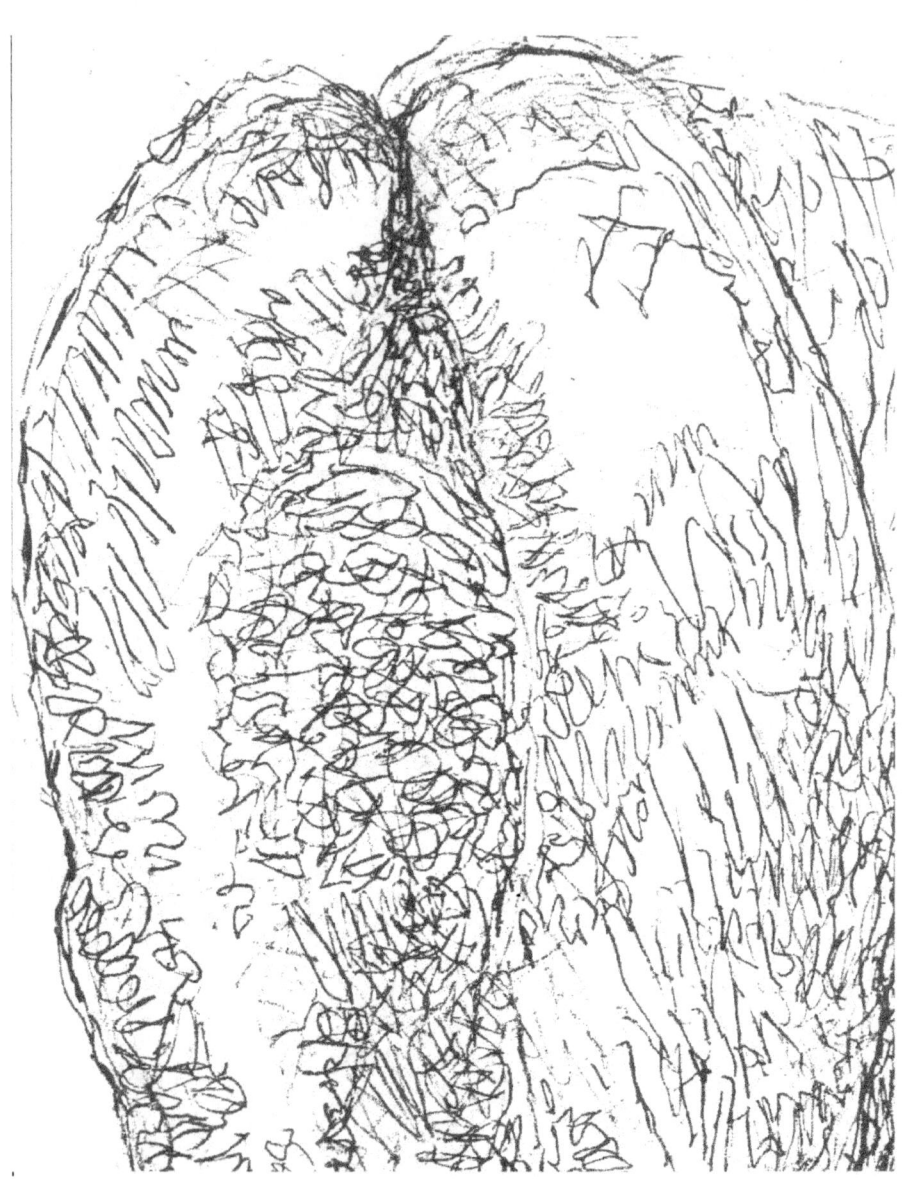

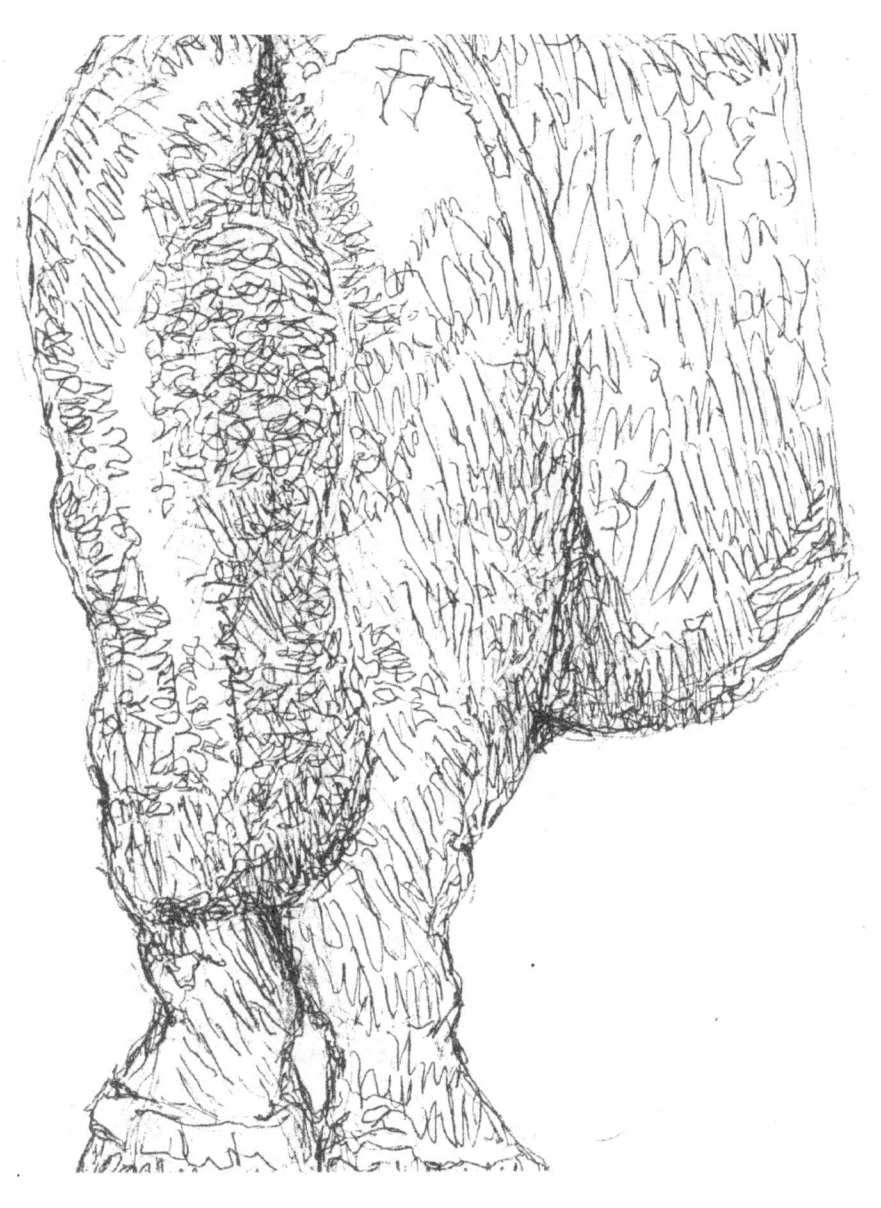

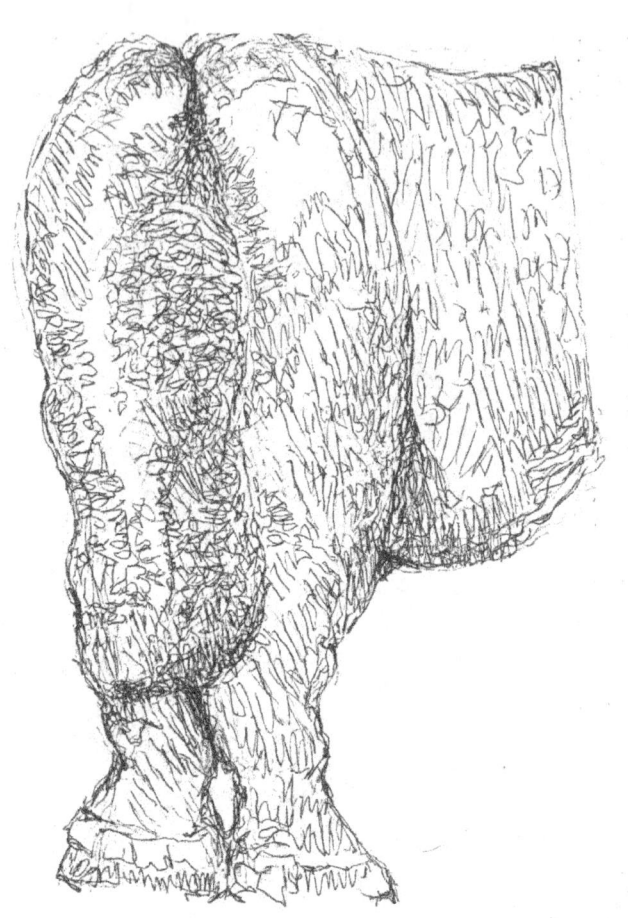

He was sworn in
and that is when
he got into the
whiskey and held
up the bank and
drank up the well
and wore out the
safe 'cause a whole
is a hole you'd
never see when
you're caught in
the act you go
down by county
"I am fiction,"
he said, "and you
can fake anything
but it 'cause it
was fake when you
first got it."
So when the judge
asked the jury he
was already gone
the best half of a
man and of course
a horse went half
into nothing of what
never was.

Say "No" If You Want It

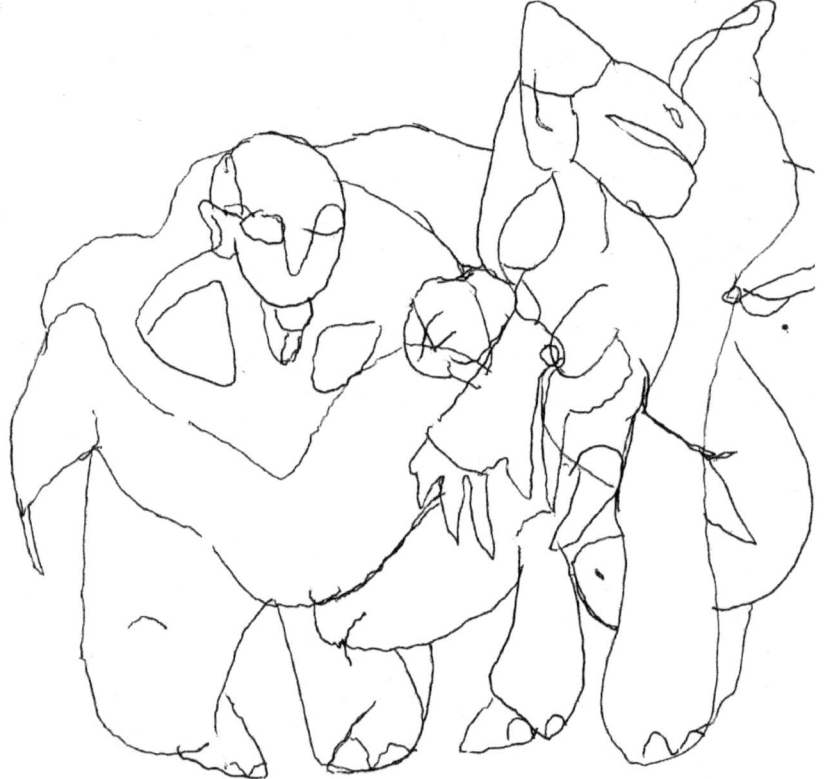

This is an impossible story to tell because like every story, not everyone is in it, and like every story, those who begin it don't begin it, and everyone in a story like this are someone else within it, and who is to say "No" they aren't until someone must.

1

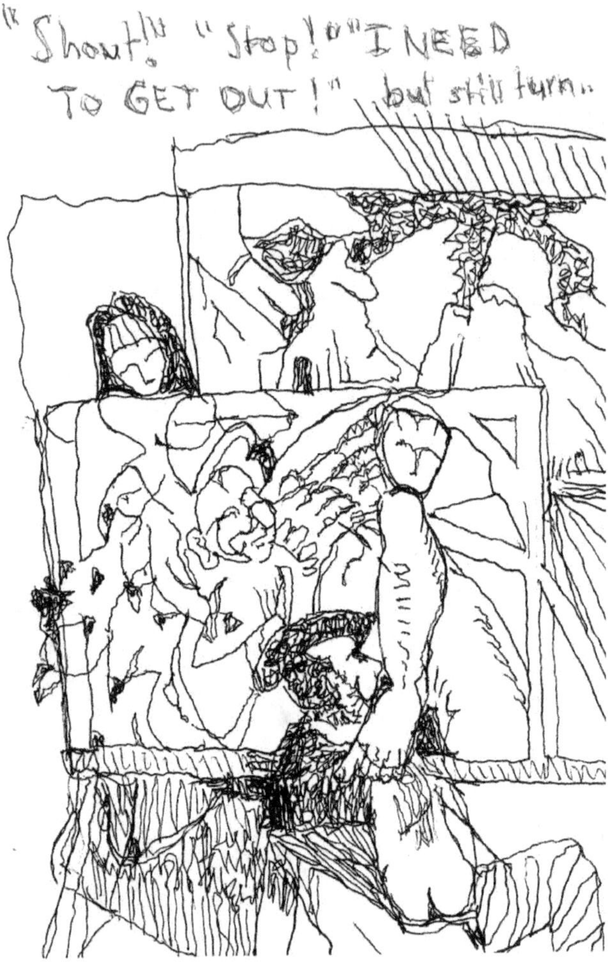
"Shout!" "Stop!" "I NEED TO GET OUT!" but still turn..

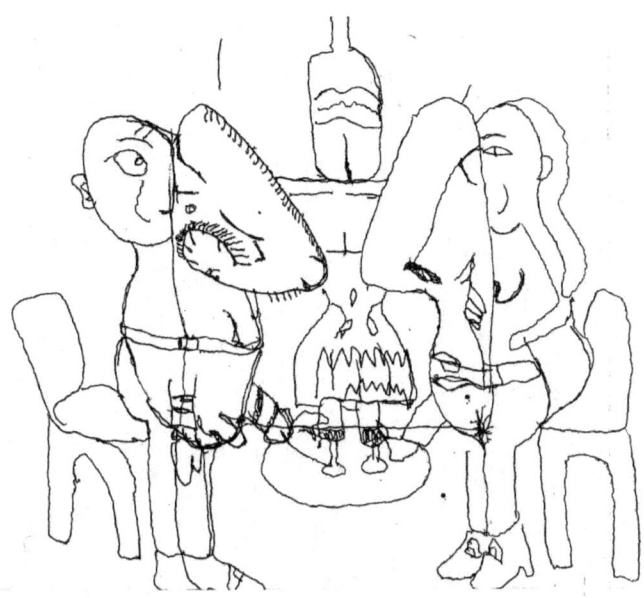

..the page. So, there was..

..this Brazillian, and this social worker on a plane..

..with Trivia who said, "I don't understand how putting less sugar in our coffee is lightening up this plane?.."

..when the stewardess said, "I just opened the door so please expect FREE fall!.."

and as they were all sucked out the Brazillian exclaimed.. "what! No More Coffee?" and the social worker said, "I don't understand the story," And Trivia said, "By the time we reach the bottom of this page none of us will have to worry."

And the stewardess said, "The fact that we are
about to be dead and all deaf from the
Fall doesn't mean that we shouldn't understand
the story at all."

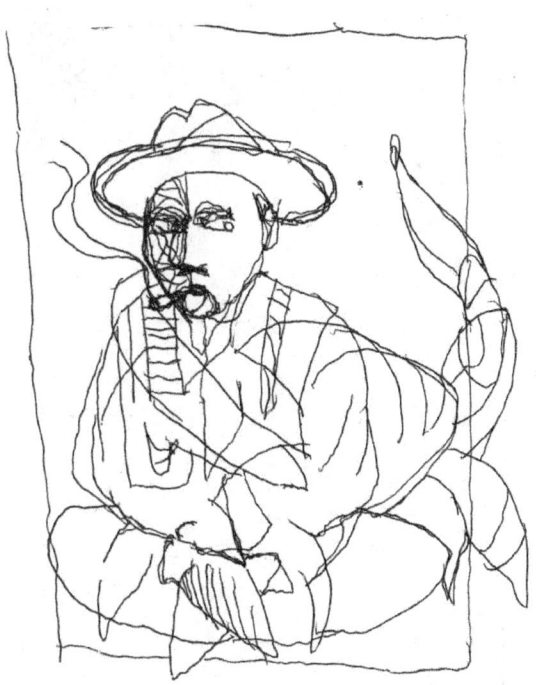

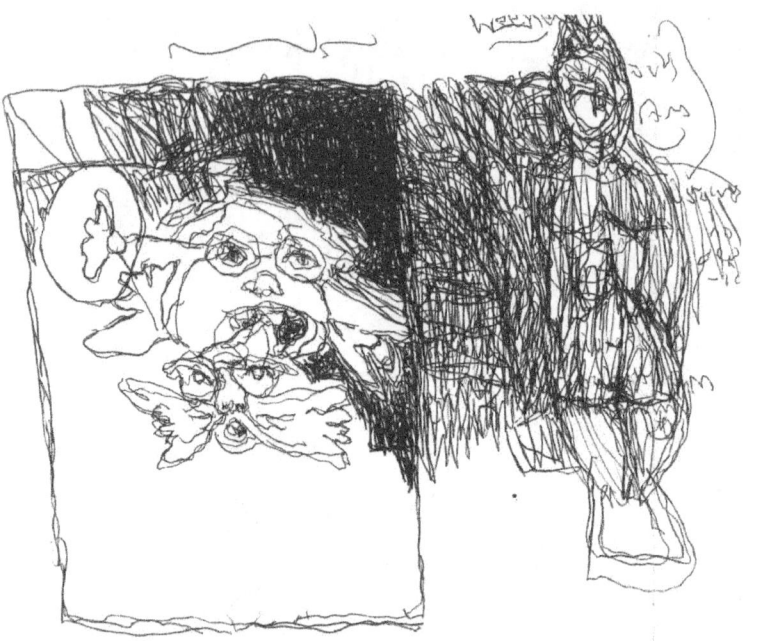

But they came down from the
sky that was dangerously high
but not high enough for
the stewardess not to be too hot to
explain," There was a scorpion and
a frog who wanted to cross
the swamp and the scorpion
said if I were to take you
over you wouldn't have
to worry that I'd sting you.

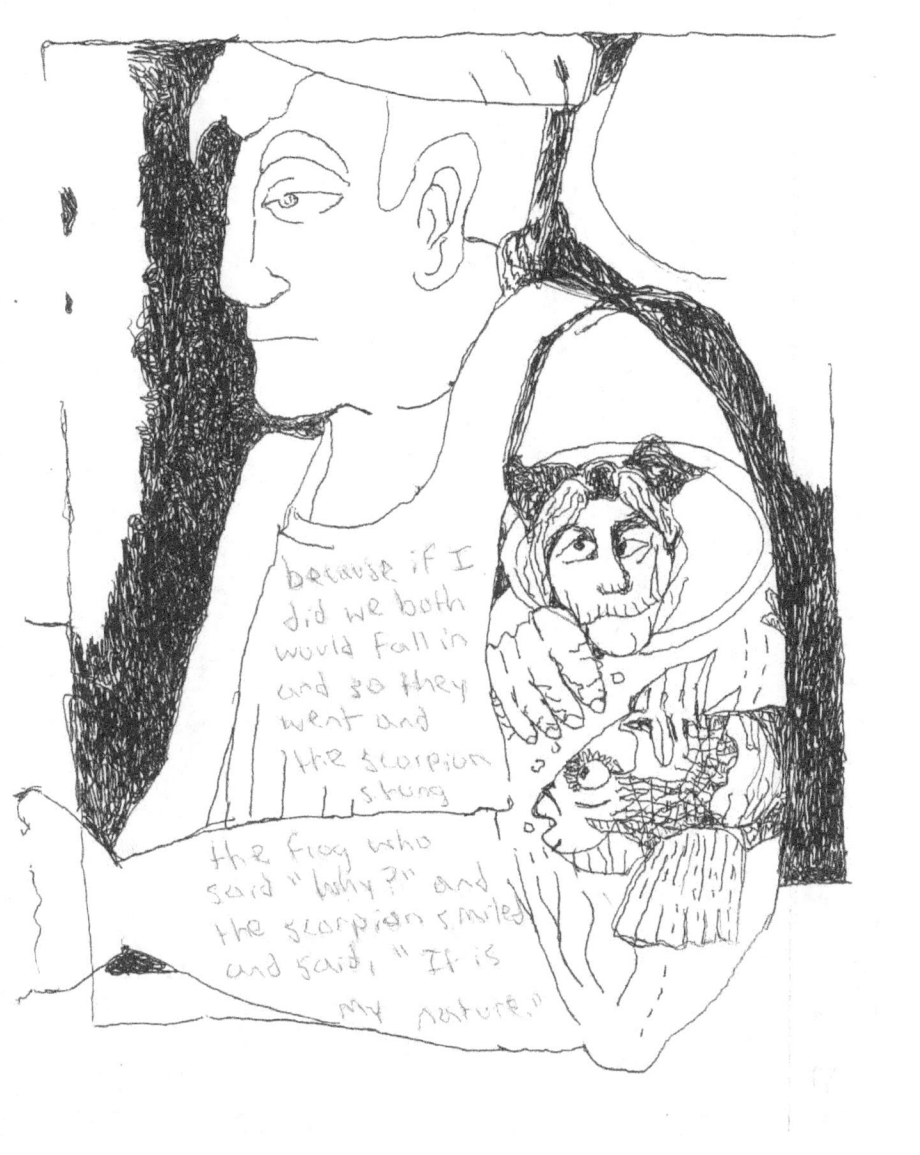

because if I
did we both
would fall in
and so they
went and
the scorpion
stung

the frog who
said "Why?" and
the scorpion smiled
and said, "It is
MY nature."

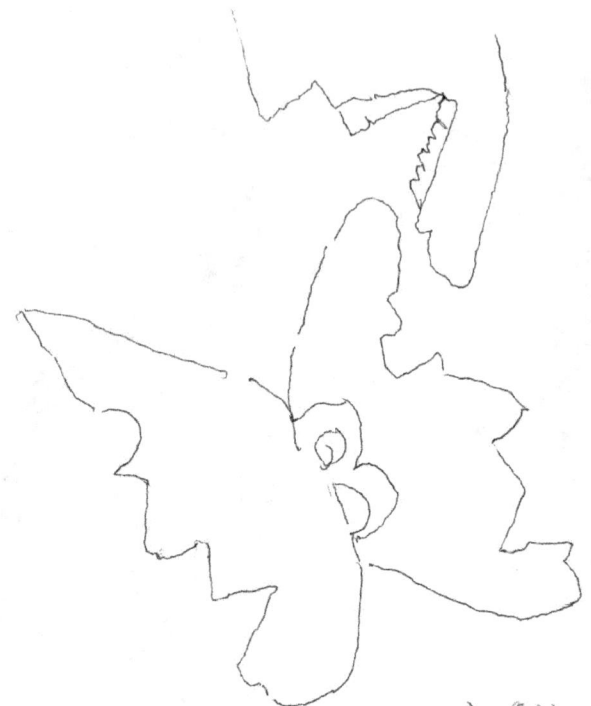

And Trivia said, "What if the scorpion was
compulsive and the frog had suicidal
ideations?"
"Then," said the doctor, "I have
another hour FREE to discuss it."
While on the carpet an iguana
gained on a leather belt because
it only knew a loophole when it
was given it. But no one cared that
it did, or prevented it including Trivia

And "It's like a Frog on a iguana crawling away
the   From a feather belt." .. "And please don't
doctor   hold up my iguana it isn't
said: a yo-yo."

When the
delivery
man came
back and said:
"Did someone order an Iguana?"
It comes FREE with a gun!"

And:
the doctor called for medication.

And Ivy asked,
"where are you From?"
while the doctor
said, " My orders
are.." and the nurse
said," Lobster?"
And the worker said,
"Newburgh Or. Canton?" and the doctor said, "Peking"
And Trivia said, "It was a score-pee-un."
And the doctor said, "No, Peking duck."
And the nurse said,   " I promise not to
look.."

And the nurse said, "Well, Say "No" if you want it medium and not well done." and the doctor said to Trivia, " "You see, if we both were fish in water and you knew there was air above us it would leave you unhappy that you couldn't dance on it and so you must submit..to this operation. " You

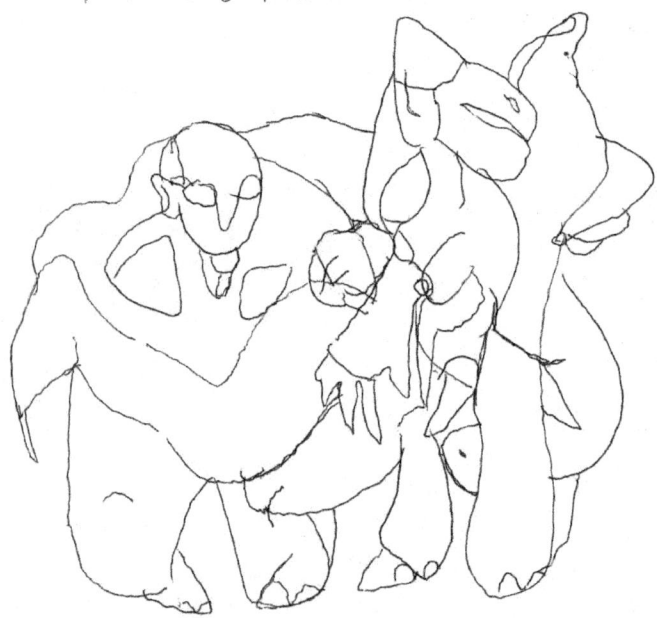

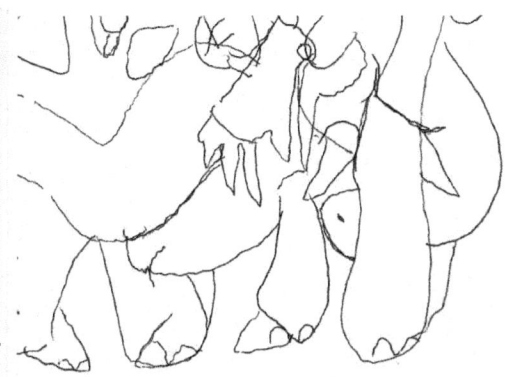

And Trivia said, "Isn't it true that some things in the water also walk on earth?"

And the judge said, "I think we've heard ample evidence that proves Trivia is harmful to others and herself."

"Wait!" said the stenographer, "Here is something else." There was Trivia shoveling snow up to her nose and a German shepard in a garter belt that said, "Say 'No' If You Want It" like how you were at 4 years old when your name was Fortune before it changed to Miss Fortune. So...

For those of you who look for "It" and say, "Hey, here 'It' is," or "What is 'It'?" or "I don't understand 'It'" the only certain thing is "It's a © infringement

"So now that I told you the story will you still eat me?" asked the fish.

"Knowing that you're myself, behind glass,
I most certainly will (Now that you asked)"
and finished "It!"

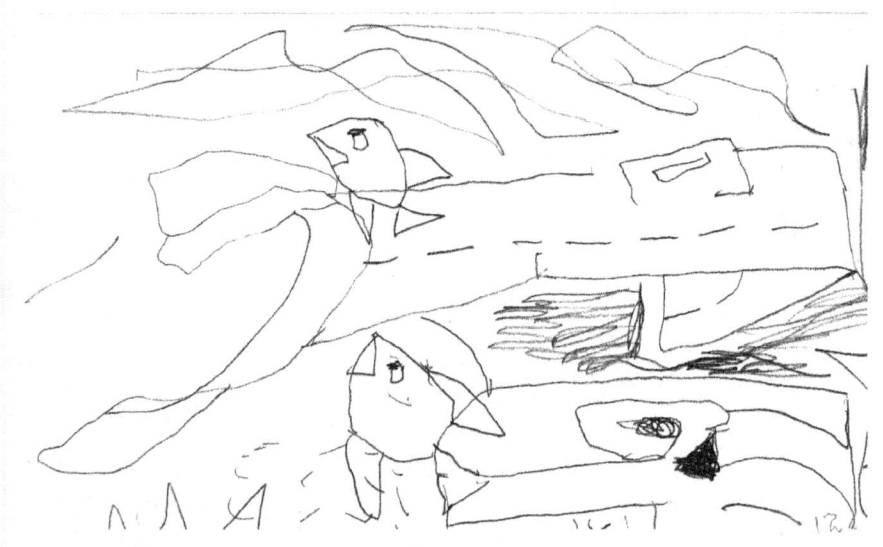

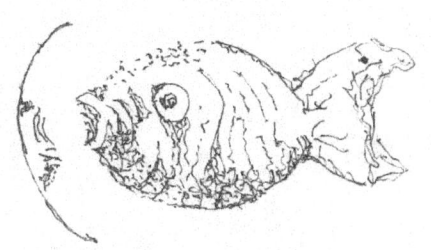

If I asked you how
could there be a
divine order? With
life as it is? If you
asked me, "Have I
seen the Levithan?"
And I said, "I have,
so turn the page and
say "No" to want what
's become of It."

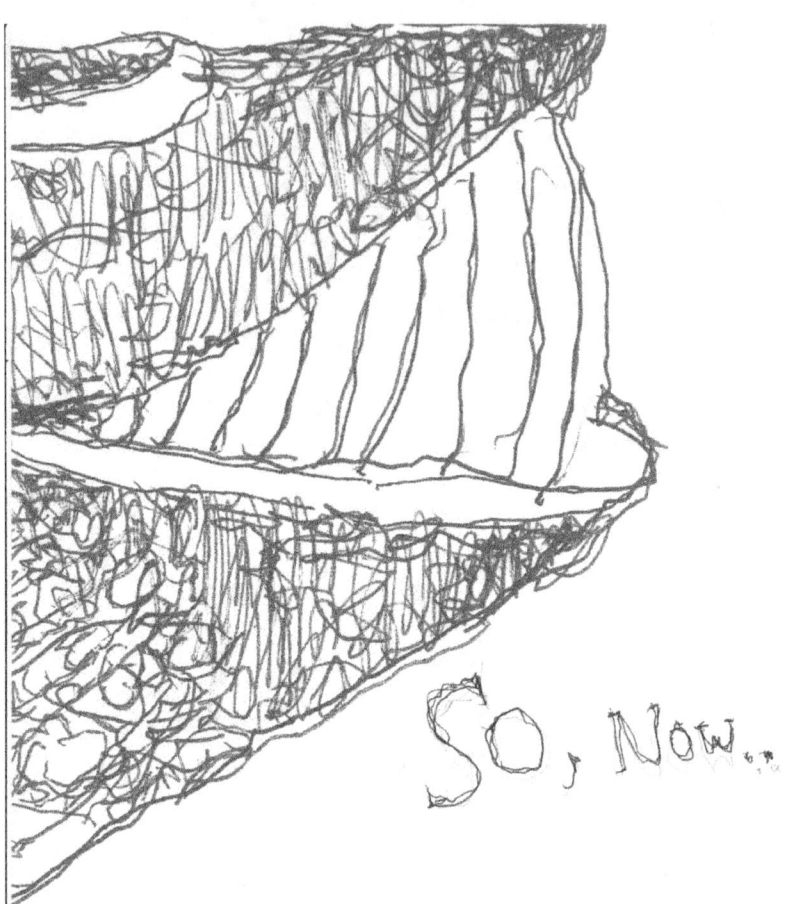

SO, NOW..

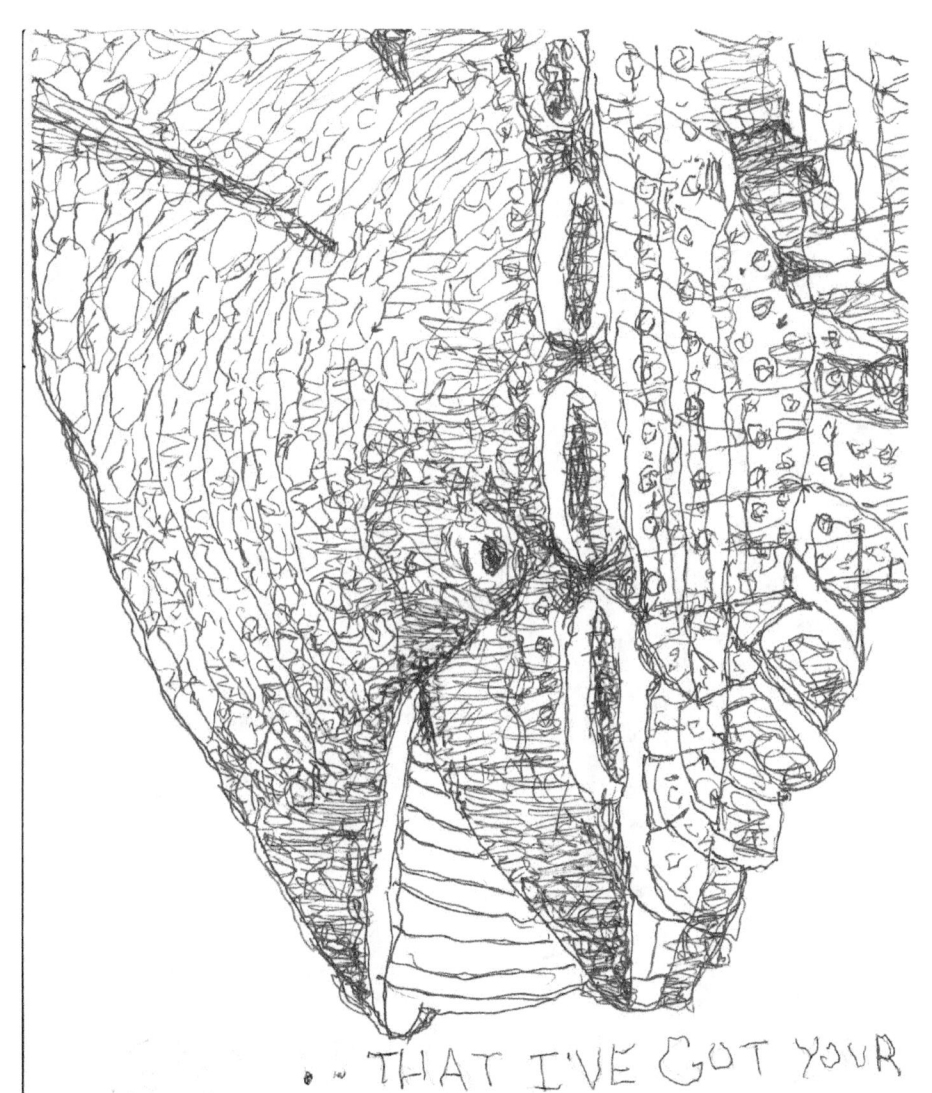

. ̃ THAT I'VE GOT YOUR

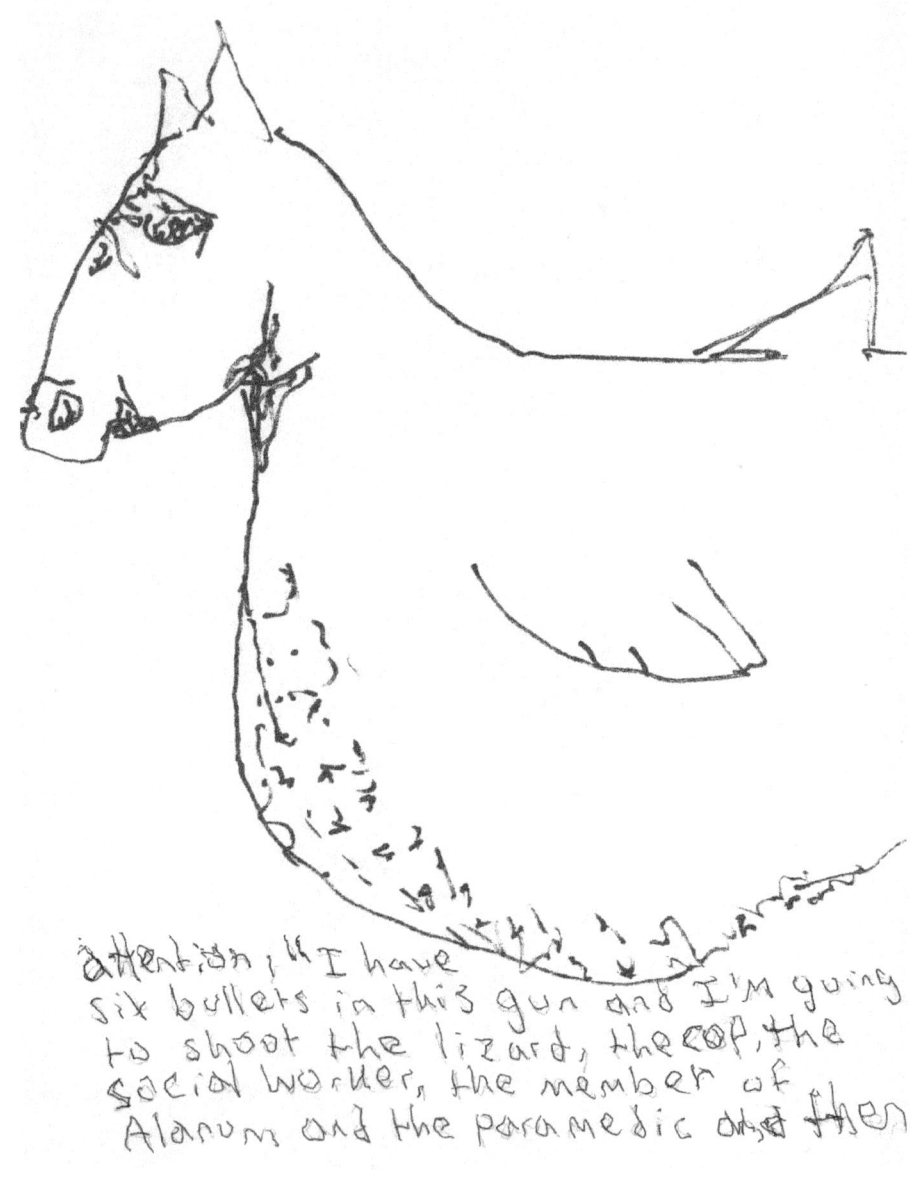

attention, "I have
six bullets in this gun and I'm going
to shoot the lizard, the cop, the
social worker, the member of
Alanon and the paramedic and then

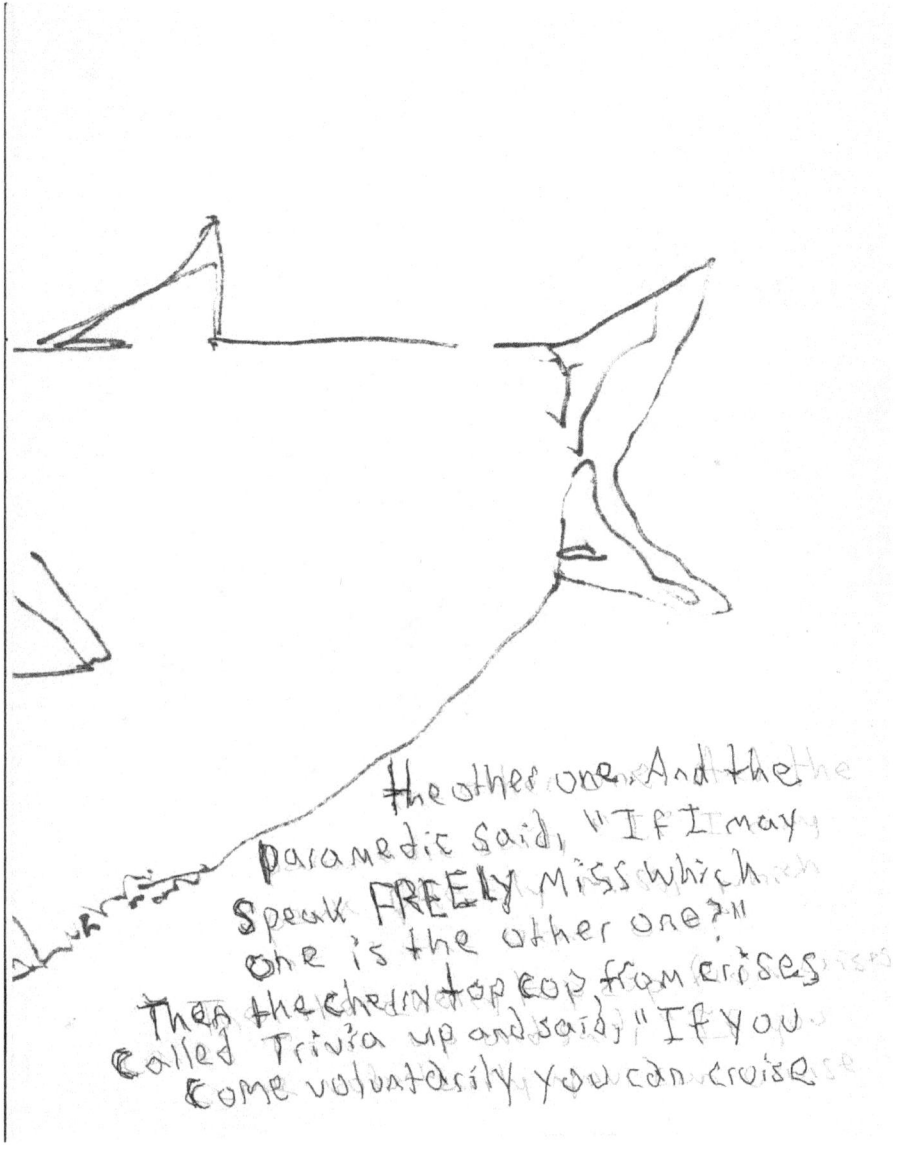

the other one. And the the
paramedic Said, "IF I may
Speak FREELY miss which
one is the other one?"
Then the chew-in-top cop from crises
Called Trivia up and said, "IF you
Come voluntarily you can cruise

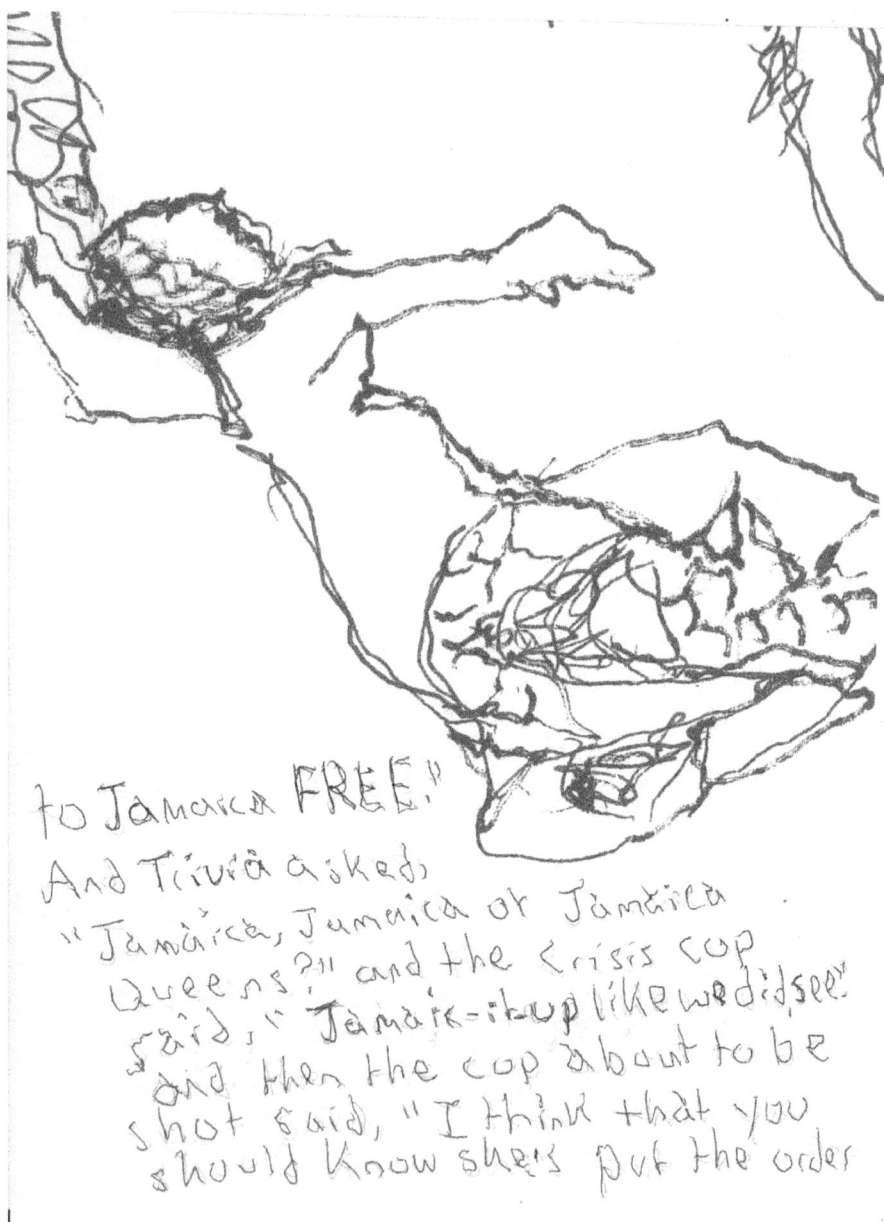

to Jamaica FREE."
And Triura asked,
"Jamaica, Jamaica or Jamaica
Queens?" and the crisis cop
said, "Jamaic-it-up like we did see"
and then the cop about to be
shot said, "I think that you
should know she's put the order

of the shooting before she ordered the
iguana that the gun comes with FREE
with delivery so before you offer there
is no iguana, she is simply
holding us by a hypothesis.
But then the paramedic said,
"Then why do I feel
tense?"
"Because," said
Trivia, "It was a
plane
and...

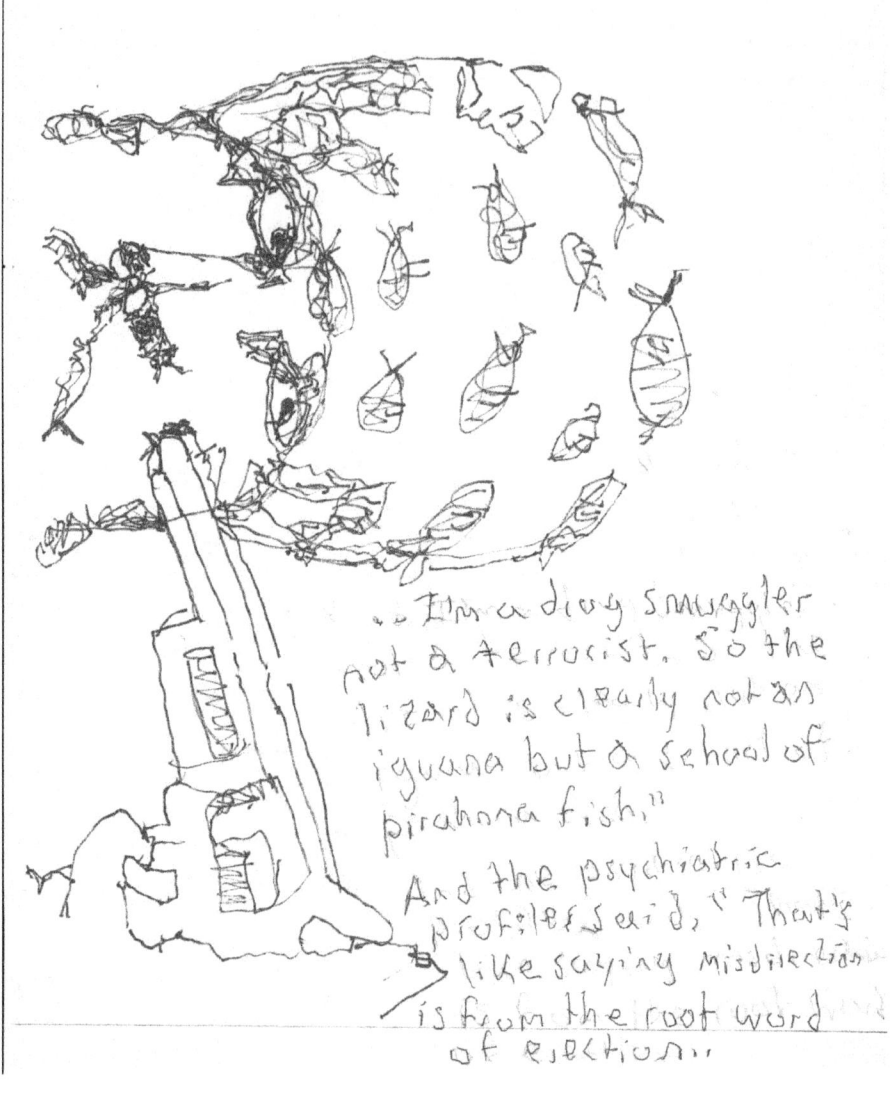

"...I'm a drug smuggler not a terrorist. So the lizard is clearly not an iguana but a school of pirahna fish."

And the psychiatric profiler said, "That's like saying misdirection is from the root word of erection..."

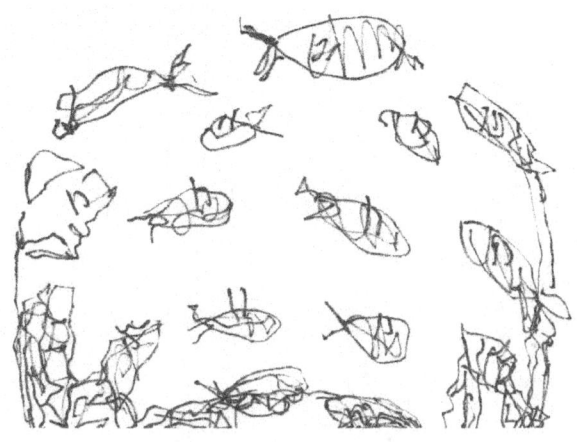

„Miss."

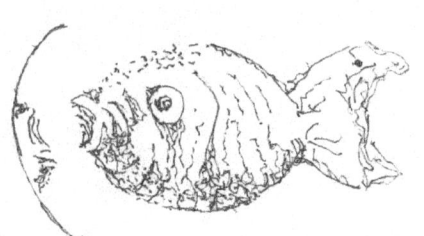

And then the medic who was tense
agreed that "IT" is, and so he was
picked out as the problem and
was offered not punishment but
A WARD for erotic Fish, and
that's where and when Trivia
ordered the iguana and was then
asked to put down the hypothetic
Then the paramedic said, "I
know my rights. I'm allowed
one call," and was told, "Yes,"
and said, "Seahorses can
change gender and we CALL
ourselves advanced!!"

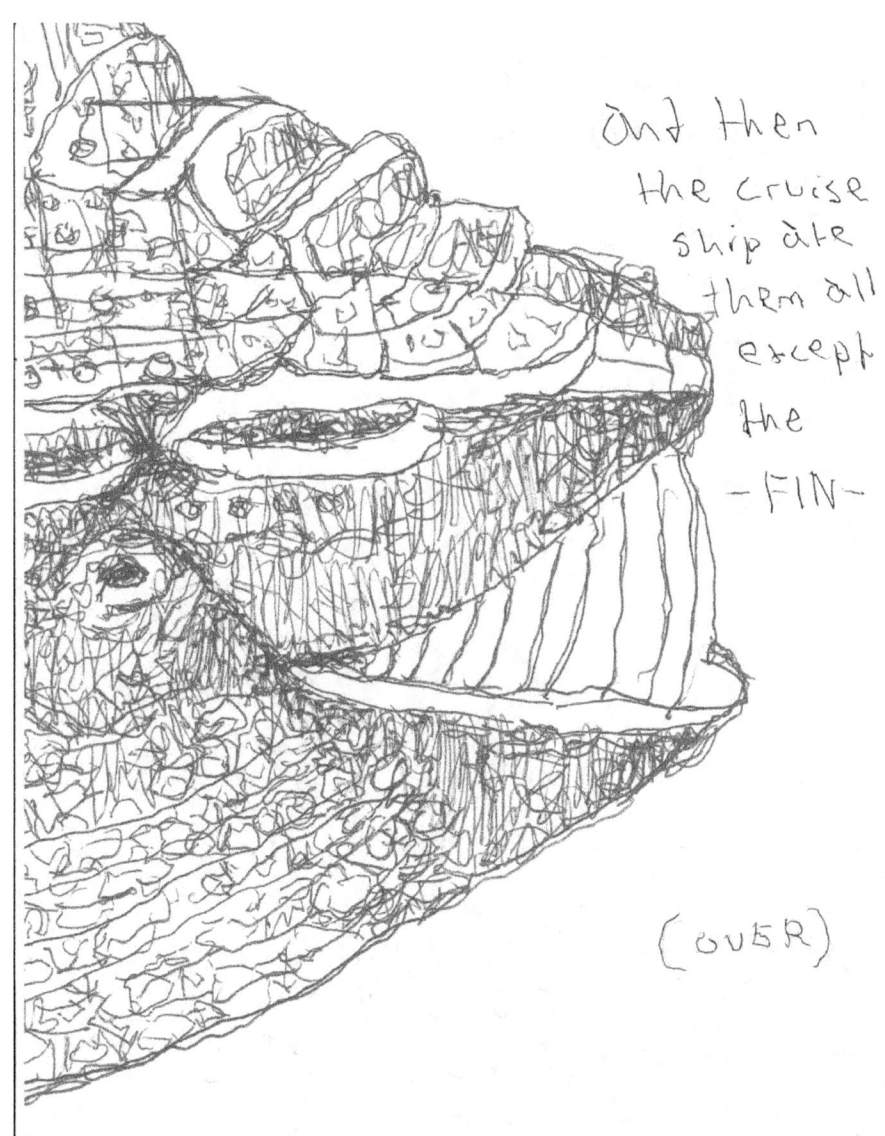

and then
the cruise
ship ate
them all
except
the
—FIN—

(OVER)

But this fin had only bee
been the word OVER inside of
of paranthesis and upon
closer   inspection...

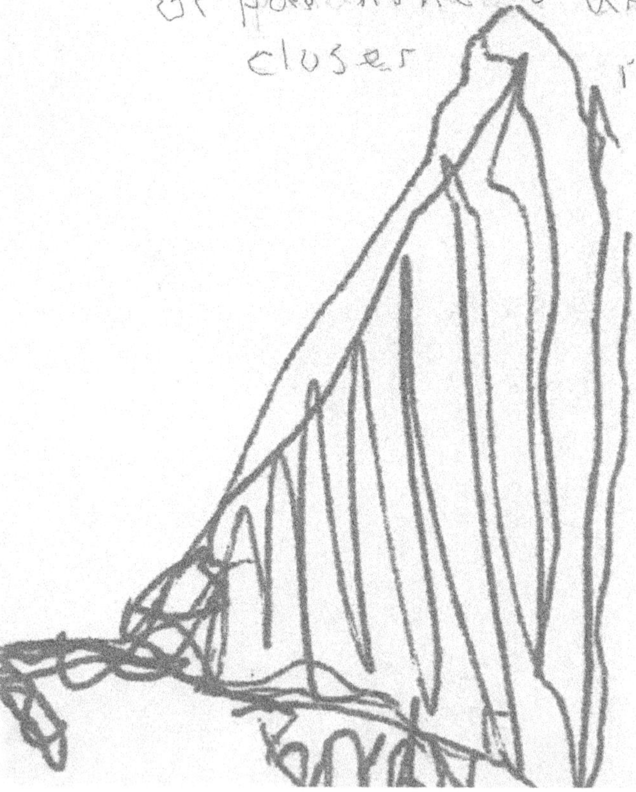

(was from here on (him)

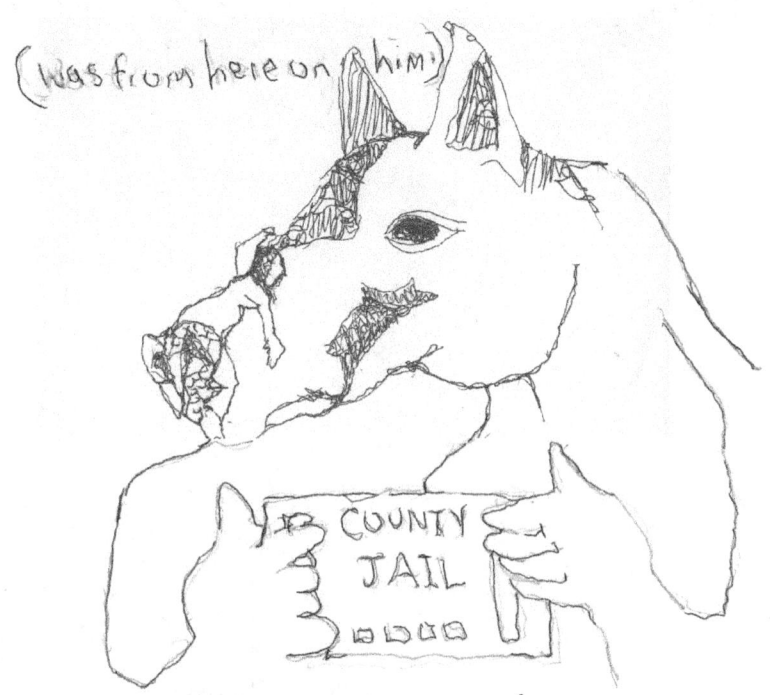

.. because the whole point of this
is in between matter and
doesn't matter, as a physicist
– might say, leaves the

coefficient of those who dwell well
on nothing and that nothing nothing
could sustain was a surprise so
for us physicists because
we were looking for a ... for ...

a star that
was similar to
OURS
while the fish
that won the Nobel
for this lives liked

frowning funhouse and
a hole taken for a ride.

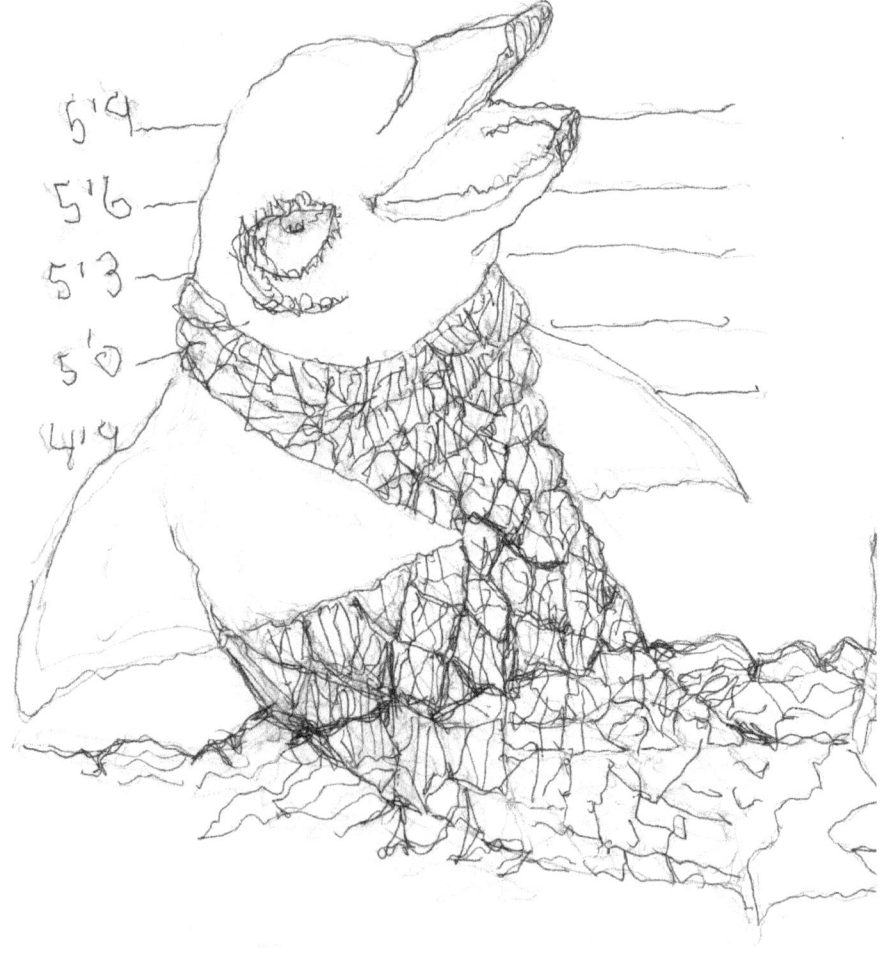

5'9
5'6
5'3
5'0
4'9

and a nibble of Mannah
dropped from the otherside.

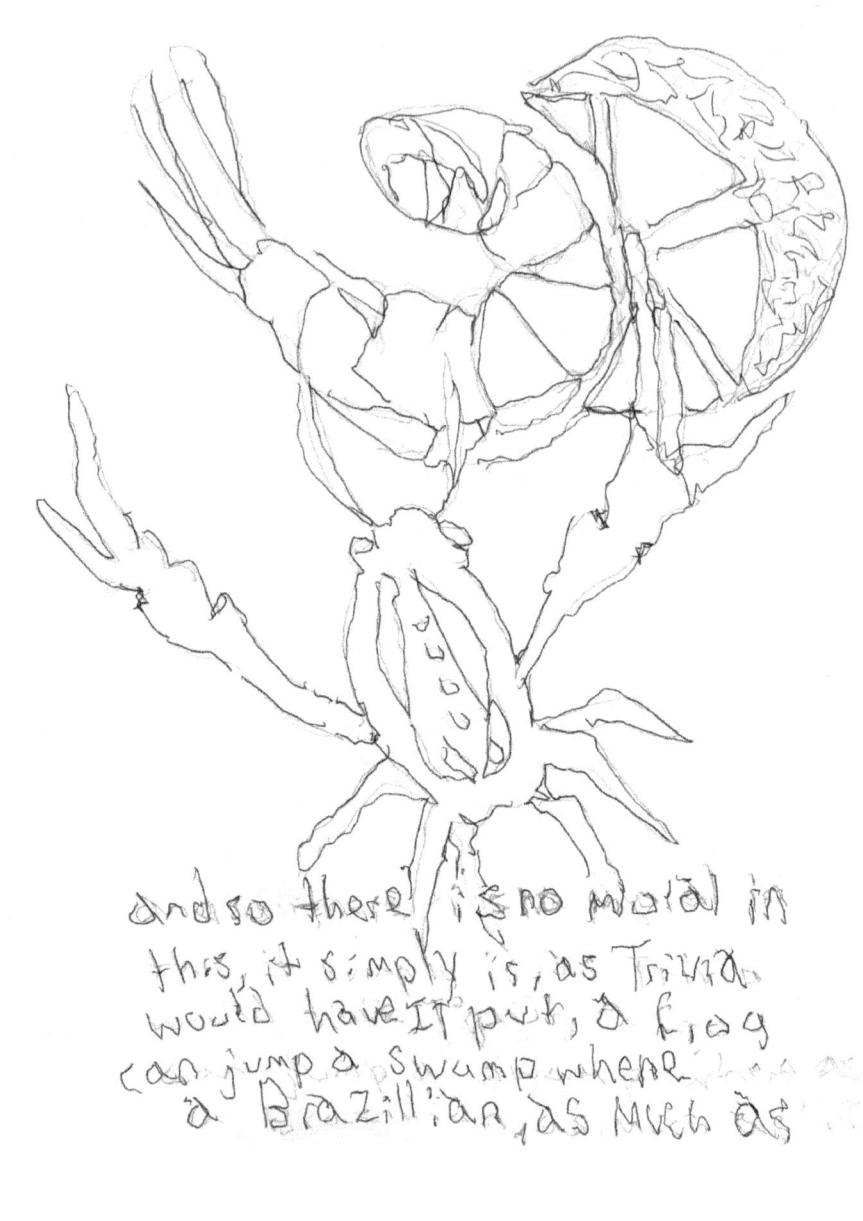

and so there is no moral in
this, it simply is, as Trivia
would have it put, a frog
can jump a swamp where
a Brazillian, as much as

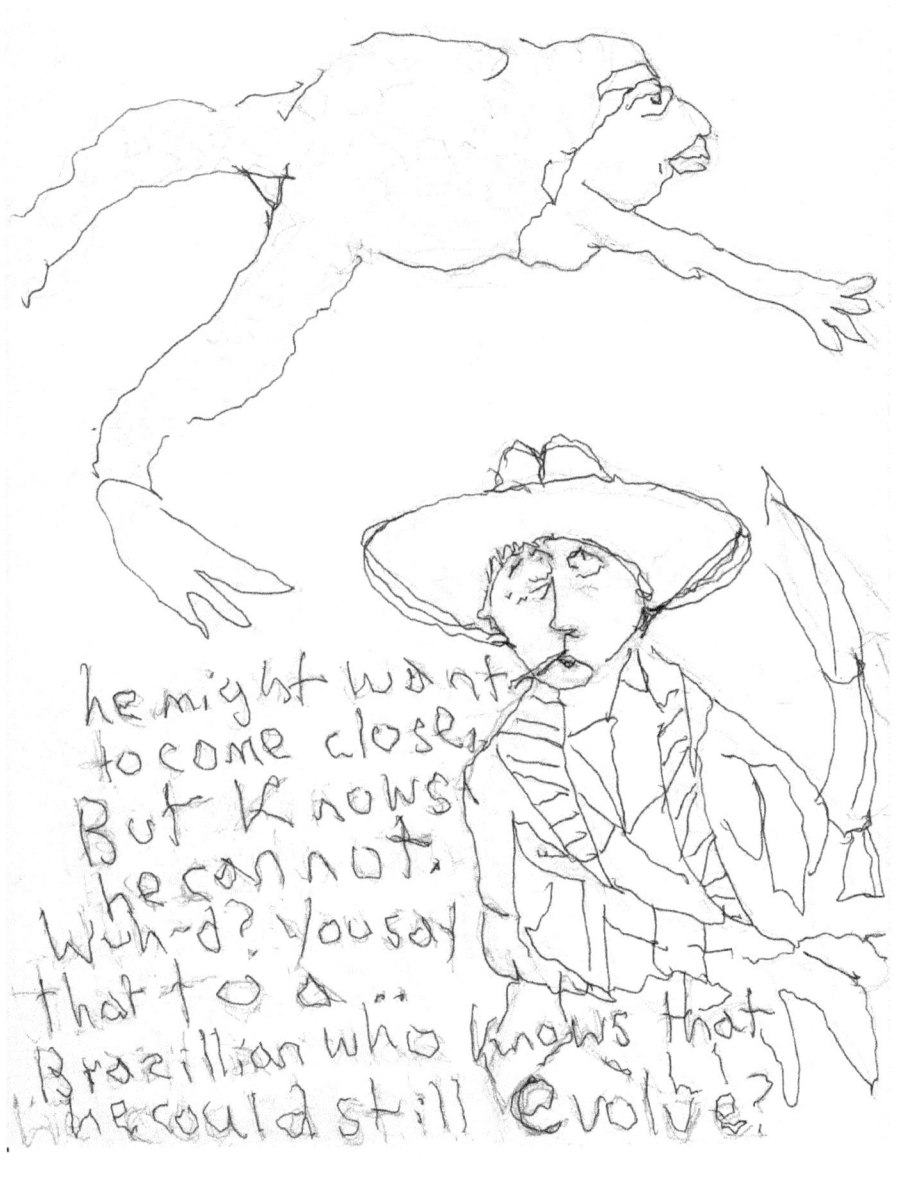

he might want
to come closer
But knows
he cannot.
Wuh-d? you say
that to a...
Brazillian who knows that
he could still evolve?

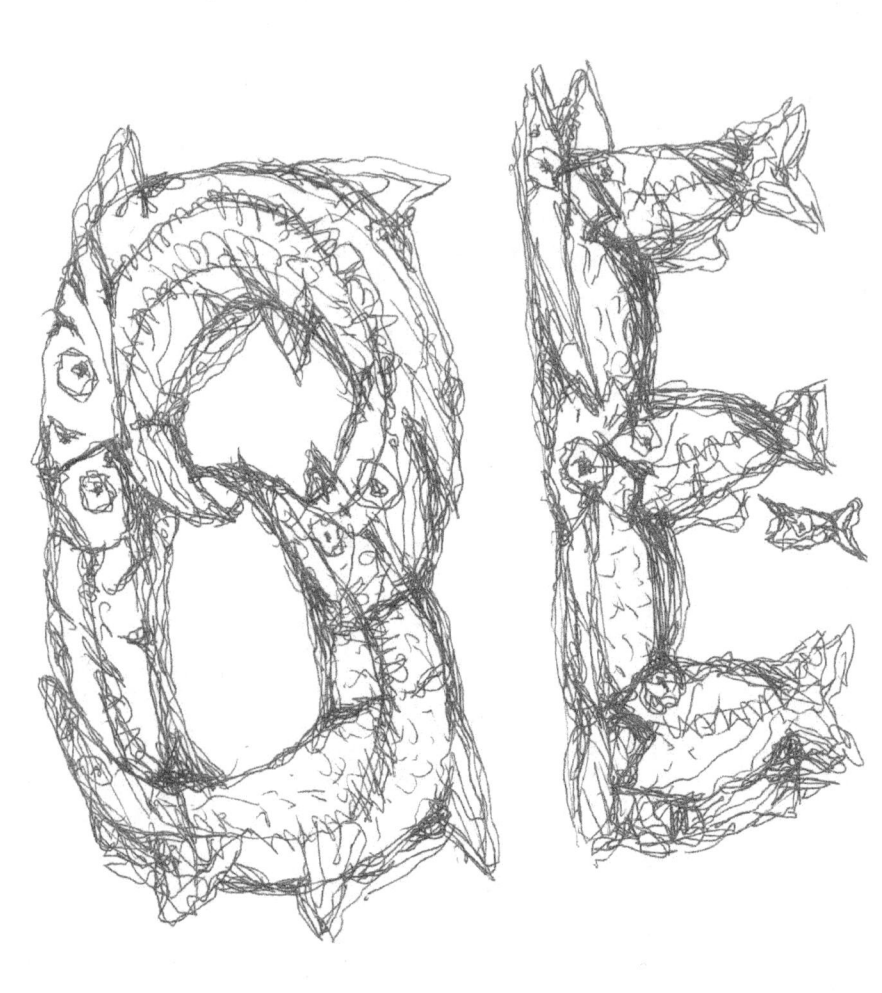

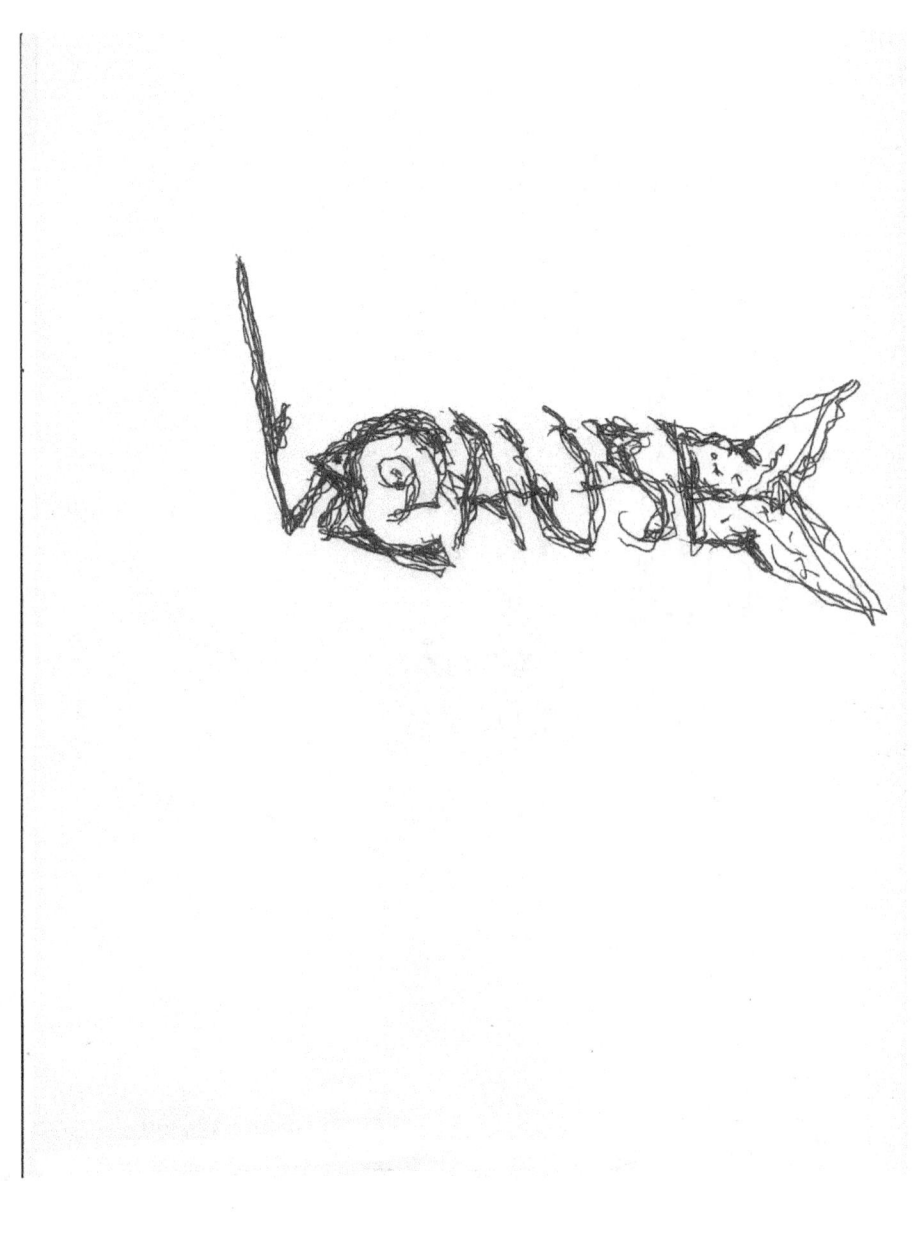

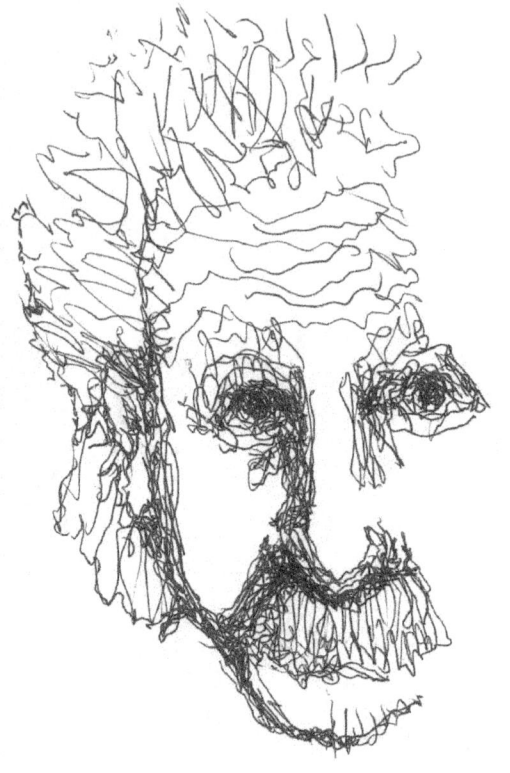

Leaps begin

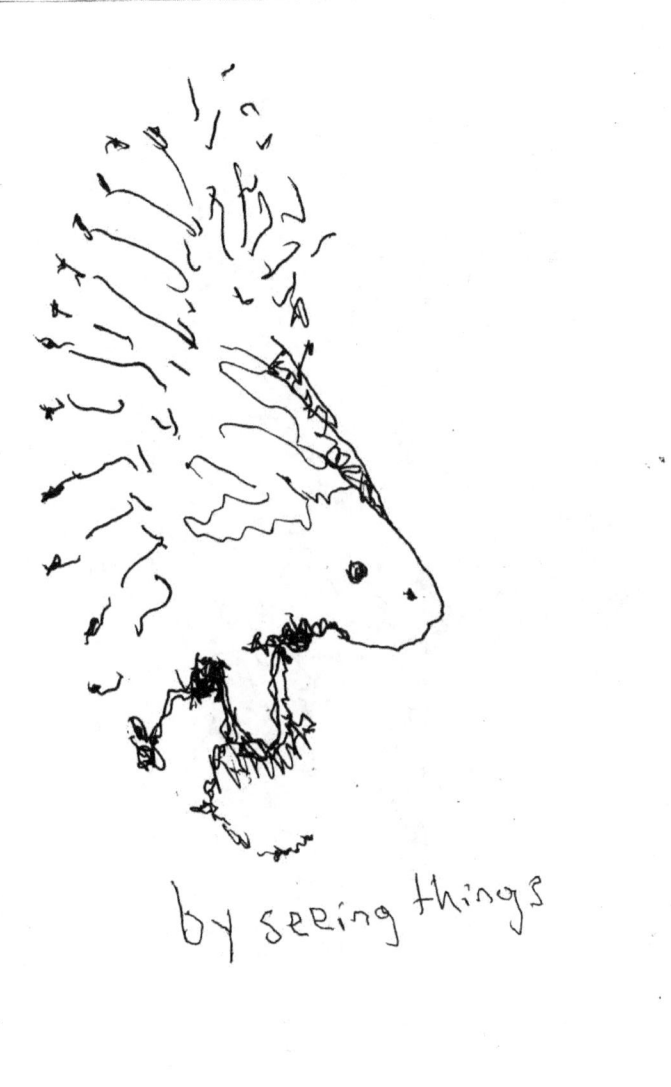

by seeing things

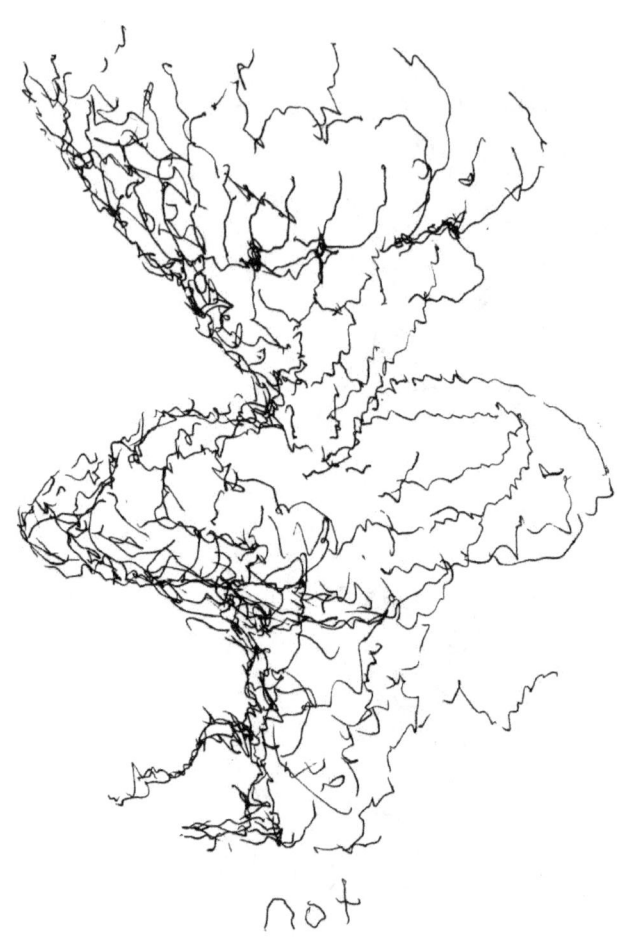

not

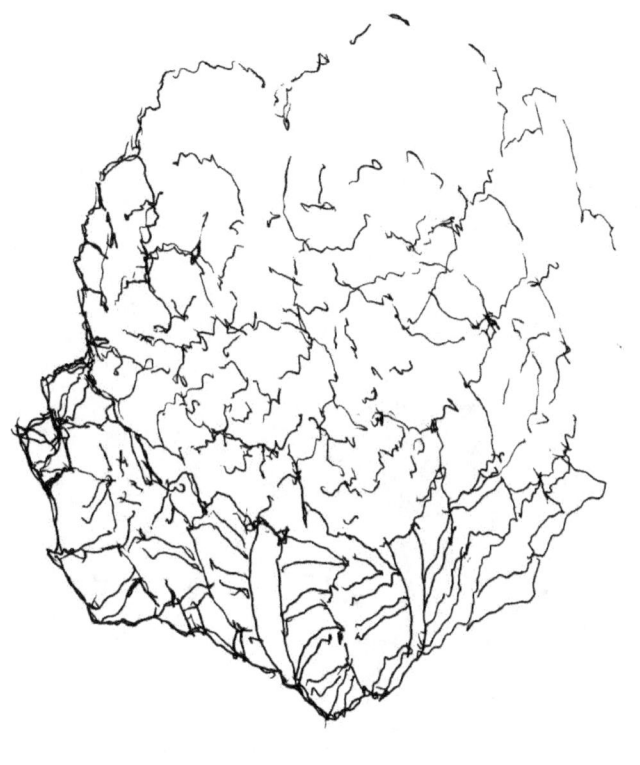

as you

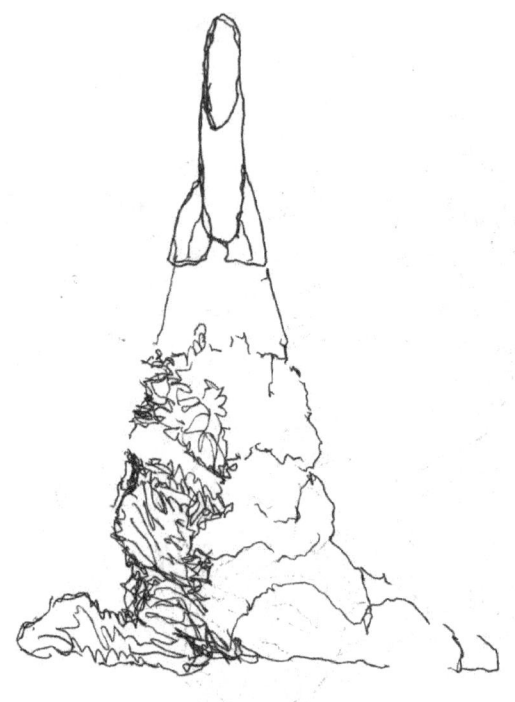

imagine them

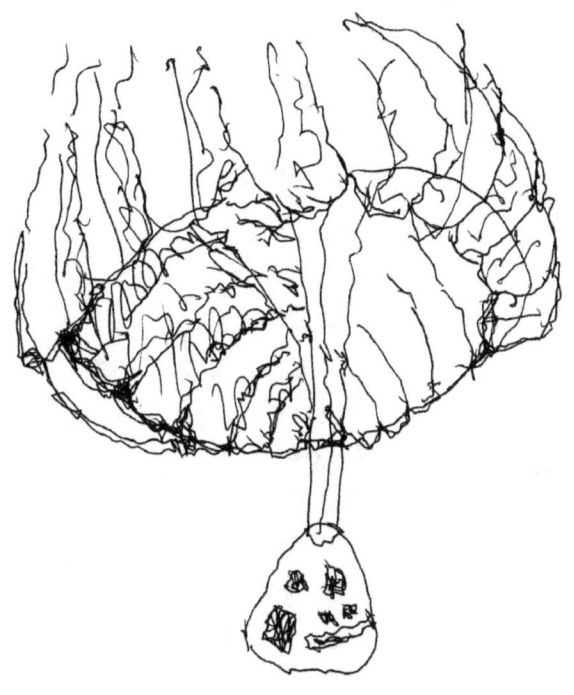

to be.

Special thanks to:
Lance Harrison
Steve Roman
Mollie and family
Roy Sidwell
The Brown sisters
C.B.
Sara
I. Chessid
S. Rees
S. Pirro
and other friends
and family.

In trying to tell
a story there
will be people
that will lie
that you should
always show and
never tell, but
what doesn't show
will always tell and
tell the most and
so the best advice
is use a picture,
have a rhyme, and
if all else fails wear
the loudest tie.

— S. Zwiren

www.ingramcontent.com/pod-product-compliance
Lightning Source LLC
Chambersburg PA
CBHW070829180526
45168CB00002B/783